THE LITTLE GIDDING WAY

THE LITTLE GIDDING WAY

Christian Community for Ordinary People

Robert Van de Weyer

Darton, Longman and Todd
London
Published in association with
Little Gidding books

First published in 1988 by
Darton, Longman and Todd Ltd
89 Lillie Road, London SW6 1UD

in association with
Little Gidding Books
Little Gidding, Huntingdon PE17 5RJ

© 1988 Robert Van de Weyer

ISBN 0 232 51780 0

British Library Cataloguing in Publication Data

Van de Weyer, Robert, *1950–*
The Little Gidding way.
1. Great Britain. Christian communities
I. Title
267′. 0941

ISBN 0–232–51780–0

Phototypeset by Input Typesetting Ltd, London SW19 8DR
Printed and bound in Great Britain by
Anchor Brendon Ltd, Tiptree, Essex

CONTENTS

'It's the right, good, old way you are in: keep in it'
Nicholas Ferrar

INTRODUCTION

Through the course of the twentieth century there have been growing numbers of Christians who have felt called to live in a close-knit community. Many have responded by remaining within their parish church, and devoting themselves to strengthening the corporate life of its people. Others have been prepared to uproot themselves, and move hundreds of miles to join a residential community. Just as the fifth century saw numerous experiments in monastic life, often going to wild extremes of spiritual heroism, so in the twentieth century innumerable small groups of Christian families have formed all over the world, inspired by the highest ideals and heroic visions. Most have lasted only a short time, as people have found themselves unable to live up to their ideals; but in the process valuable lessons have been learnt.

Now, as we move towards the twenty-first century, God seems to be guiding us towards more stable, and perhaps less adventurous, forms of community life, in which ordinary families and single people can share. Yet this presents fresh challenges of its own. Not only must we learn from the recent experiments, but we must look further back into Christian history to discover the art of stable community life. After their own period of experiment the monasteries found a pattern of life which has proved remarkably durable, and over the centuries millions of quite ordinary men and women have served God as monks and nuns. The Reformation of the sixteenth century was nurtured by small communities of families, mainly in central Europe, seeking to imitate the life of the first Christians of Jerusalem; and the Reformation itself inspired many new communities throughout Europe, including Britain.

1

My own call to community came through my conversion to Christianity itself. In 1970 I lived for nine months in a small community in South India whose members belonged to the ancient Orthodox Church of India, dating right back to the third century. It was through living with a group who sought to apply the gospel to every aspect of their lives that I became convinced of the truth of the gospel; and in becoming a Christian I knew that my own vocation was to live within a similar community in my own country. To prepare myself I devoted much of the following years to studying the history of Christian community. I looked in detail at the main western tradition of monastic life founded by St Benedict; and also spent a year visiting monasteries in Ethiopia, where the earliest pattern of monastic community, founded by St Pachomius in the Egyptian desert, had continued virtually unchanged for fifteen centuries – it was also the pattern that the early Celtic monasteries of Britain adopted.

These studies eventually led to Little Gidding, a remote hamlet west of Huntingdon where a tiny chapel and an old farmhouse stand isolated amidst gently rolling countryside. There in the early seventeenth century Nicholas Ferrar founded a community, based on his own extended family, which lasted about thirty years. I had read about Little Gidding even before becoming a Christian, and had camped there for a fortnight in 1972. Then five years later my wife Sarah and I, with our two small children, moved there, raising money for a charitable trust to purchase the farmhouse, outbuildings and eight acres of land. We converted the outbuildings into houses for new community members, and within a few years about twenty-five people – single people, married couples and children – were living there. In 1981 the Community of Christ the Sower was formed when those at Little Gidding made a formal covenant one to another.

It had always been our intention that the Community would not be confined to Little Gidding but would have other branches in ordinary villages and towns. I had often dreamt that the first branch would be at Leighton Bromswold, where the poet George Herbert had restored the church – and where my own ancestors, George Herbert's patrons, had built the small manor house next to the church in 1616. George Herbert was a close friend of Nicholas Ferrar, and was inspired by the community at Little Gidding; so when he became a country parson he, with his wife Jane, formed a community based on the parish in which he ministered. Our opportunity came in 1985 when the manor house was offered for sale: we purchased it, and Sarah and I moved there, with other members of the Community living in houses in the village. So, within a single community, we now incorporate the two main forms of community life: the residential group in which people are gathered on a single site, and the parish community in which the members are scattered within the neighbourhood, but share many aspects of their lives.

This book is our Rule of Life – or, more precisely, a guide for our life together. We do not have a strict rule in the monastic sense, in which every part of our life is governed by a written document. Rather we have four simple prayers which express our common vision; and this book is about how we try to put that vision into practice. The four prayers introduce the four chapters of the book: Covenant, Stewardship, Ministry, and Reconciliation. And the chapters are divided into twelve sections, each devoted to one phrase of the prayer.

I have called the book *The Little Gidding Way* in memory of the words of Nicholas Ferrar, shortly before his death, when he handed over the leadership of the community to his brother John: 'It is the right, good, old way you are in; keep in it.' We, too, know there is nothing new in our way of life, and that when we make mistakes it is invariably because we have failed to learn the lessons of the past. So in this book I frequently refer to our spiritual forbears who have taught us how to live in community: to Nicholas Ferrar and George Herbert; to the Benedictine monasteries of the West and the Pachomian monasteries of the East; and above all, to the first Christian community formed at Pentecost in Jerusalem, described in the Acts of the Apostles.

Yet although the essence of Christian community never changes, its outward expression is constantly evolving; and today the call to community is being heard more widely than ever before. In the past only a tiny minority of Christians have belonged to communities; today the movement towards community seems to be stirring people throughout the Church, and is in all sorts of ways – seen and unseen, large and small – affecting people's way of life and worship. So I have subtitled the book 'Christian Community for Ordinary People'.

Like any community rule, this one is written for a particular community, The Community of Christ the Sower. But I hope it will be of interest to a much wider audience: to the many people who are wondering about forming new communities; and to the far greater number who feel their own parish church is called to be more communal. The challenges – and the pitfalls – are the same for us all, and the wisdom acquired through trial and error in one group can readily be applied elsewhere. I doubt if anyone will agree with everything written here; but I do hope that it will seem realistic and practical – and that people who regard themselves as quite ordinary and unheroic will feel better able to respond to the challenge of Christian community.

COVENANT

As God has established a new covenant with his people in Jesus Christ, we pray that we may be seeds of his kingdom on earth.

We commit ourselves to one another as fellow disciples of Christ, worshipping him together in prayer and in action.

God binds us together in mutual trust, that we may support one another through warm and tender friendship.

May we be loyal and steadfast partners in his service, cherishing one another both in sorrow and in joy.

God has made us members one of another with Christ as our head, that we may be joined together in common vision and purpose.

May we receive graciously into our midst those whom God sends, growing as one body in his love.

As God has established a new covenant with his people in Jesus Christ . . .

The Community of Christ the Sower is a tiny twig at the end of a branch of a tree whose roots lie in the first Christian church in Jerusalem. After Pentecost the first Christians immediately formed a close-knit community: they prayed together daily; they frequently celebrated communion and shared meals; and they pooled all their possessions, distributing them to each person according to their need. The close fellowship they enjoyed attracted others, and people joined the church in large numbers.

We are not told how long the community lasted. But quite soon, from this common root, two main branches of church

5

life emerged. The first, and numerically by far the most important, was what we would now call the parish church. Christians live in ordinary homes and work in the world, coming together once a week for worship and perhaps for a few additional meetings. Thus they guide and support one another in trying to live out the gospel in normal jobs and neighbourhoods. The second was the monastery in which single men or women live together in a community cut off from the world, so that the whole of their daily life is subject to the commands of the gospel. The first monastic communities, founded by Pachomius in the Eygptian desert, were free associations of men who had been living as hermits. About a century later Benedict founded a monastery near Rome, and wrote the monastic rule which gave clear and strict orders to govern every aspect of the monk's life; and as monasticism spread through the western church, Benedict's Rule was widely adopted.

In addition there has been a third, much smaller branch of Christian corporate life that has blossomed intermittently through the centuries: families and single people together, still involved in the world, yet living in closer community than is possible in the ordinary parish church. The Third Orders, founded by Francis and Dominic in the thirteenth century, were an attempt to formulate a rule of life appropriate to people in every circumstance. It was this same vision which inspired Cranmer and the English reformers who compiled the Book of Common Prayer. They rewrote the old monastic offices as two short services, Morning and Evening Prayer, to be used as the daily worship of the whole church. Thus the life of shared prayer should no longer be the special preserve of monks and nuns, but was for ordinary people coming together in their homes or local church. This vision of spiritual community for ordinary people lay at the heart of the English Reformation; and, although it was frequently lost in the political and religious conflicts of the time, it continued to inspire new generations.

In particular two young men in the early seventeenth century, Nicholas Ferrar and George Herbert, sought in their different circumstances to put it into practice. They were contemporaries at Cambridge, where they both had successful academic careers; Nicholas then went into his family business while George Herbert entered politics, and they were both briefly Members of Parliament in 1624. But two years later they had each turned their back on politics and business, retreating into the remote countryside to form simple communities of prayer. Nicholas Ferrar went to Little Gidding where, with other members of his family, he established a large household with married couples, children and single people living together. George Herbert initially took the living at Leighton Bromswold, five miles from Little Gidding, where with the Ferrars' help he restored the beautiful church; he then married and went to Bemerton near Salisbury, where as a country parson he drew others within the parish to share in his daily devotions. They saw themselves as pursuing the same goal, of creating Christian community in which ordinary people could share, but seeking it in complementary ways. While Nicholas Ferrar created a residential group, like a monastery, George Herbert lived a similar life within a normal parish.

Since then, and especially from the early years of the twentieth century, there have been numerous experiments in community life for families. Sadly few have survived, many collapsing within a short time, mainly because they have been too tight and close-knit in their pattern of life, and too high in their ideals. Yet the call of community grows in strength, with increasing numbers of families and single people seeking to commit themselves to some form of common life. We are simply a small group of people who have received and responded to this call. We must seek to be true to the original vision of community embodied in the Jerusalem church, in the monasteries and in the way of life of our founders, Nicholas Ferrar and George Herbert. If we are willing to learn humbly from our forebears, then our little twig will be secure and firm on the tree of Christian community; and in God's way and in his time we will blossom, and be seeds of his kingdom in the world.

. . . we pray that we may be seeds of his kingdom on earth

At the heart of the Christian life there is tension between vision and practice, ideal and reality. On the one hand in following Christ we are committed to the total, uncompromising love of the Sermon on the Mount, in which we are to hold nothing back; and we are to put that love into practice in our common life, as the first Christians in Jerusalem did. On the other hand in our ordinary everyday lives we seem constantly forced to accept lower, shabbier standards, because we find ourselves unable to live up to Christ's commands; and our churches and communities seem like murky shadows of the life of the Jerusalem Christians.

The monks who went out into the desert sought to resolve this tension by withdrawing from the world, and establishing societies in which every aspect was in accordance with Christ's gospel. The astonishingly rapid spread of monasticism, to Ethiopia in the far south-east of the Christian world and to the British Isles in the far north-west, bore witness to the powerful attraction of its high ideals. And monastic communities dotted round the countryside were the main means of carrying the gospel to both Britain and Ethiopia, as well as to many other countries. Yet from the outset the monasteries evoked resentment. The church authorities, increasingly involved in the political and economic affairs of the world, saw monasticism as a living judgement on their greed and corruption. More fundamentally, many sincere Christians to this day regard monastic life as an escape from the true mission of the Church, which is to apply the values of the gospel to society itself.

The parish church has to try and resolve the tension between vision and practice in the opposite way to that of a monastery. It offers teaching and worship each Sunday in which the vision is expressed in word and symbol; and during the rest of the week the individual seeks to live out the gospel as best he can in his family, neighbourhood and place of work. There is frequently no choice but to accept compromise, not in the sense of being immoral oneself, but participating in institutions whose standards fall far short of the Christian ideal. Parish life is the pattern for the great majority of Chris-

8

tians; and, for all its limitations, it can nurture deep spiritual insight and holiness.

Our way of life stands between that of the monastery and the parish; and, as a consequence, far from resolving the tension between vision and practice, we live with it daily. Those of us with ordinary jobs outside the community can feel acutely the contrast between the standards we apply in making decisions at work, and those in making community decisions. Our children attend ordinary schools, and from an early age become aware of the differences between the life of the villages and towns where their school-friends live, and life within the community. We watch television, visit the theatre and cinema, go shopping in nearby towns; yet like monks we are committed to a rule of life, involving not only prayer, but also a strict discipline of material stewardship. Day by day our Christian ideal and harsh reality collide.

It is tempting to try and avoid this collision by veering to one side or the other; but both spell the destruction of our community. At times the isolation of the monastery seems to beckon. We want to withdraw from the world, and even perhaps to set up special schools within the community for our children, so they too can remain insulated from worldly influences. We desire to make the community materially and socially self-sufficient, every hour of the day and every aspect of our lives bound up within it, so outside contact seems unnecessary. At other times the community itself can seem dull and stifling, its demands a great weight on our shoulders, and life in the world can seem free and exciting by contrast. So we begin to treat the community with contempt, and regard the details of its life as trivial and beneath our concern. Either way we shall be unfaithful to our true vocation.

Our calling is to live in the gap between vision and practice, ideal and reality. We have not chosen it; God chose it for us. And, in remaining faithful to our call, we shall bear witness to Christ's gospel in a way that many, to whom both monasteries and parish churches seem strange and incomprehensible, can understand. In the present age monasteries seem too remote from people's normal lives, while the life of Christians within ordinary parishes can seem to an outside observer barely distinguishable from that of their neighbours without faith. Our life is sufficiently distinct from the world to make manifest, in some small measure, the gospel vision. And our life is sufficiently normal and involved in worldly concerns that people can readily see how their lives also can be transformed by this vision.

We commit ourselves to one another as fellow disciples of Christ . . .

We each belong to a number of communities. The most important is our family; and beyond that a network of relatives and friends. We are each members of a church with its own traditions, making particular demands on our time and resources. We are part of a local community, with its schools, playgroups, social meetings, and political affairs. And we belong to a nation and to human society as a whole, so that no desperate need, such as famine or war, however remote it may be, is beyond our care and concern.

Membership of the Community of Christ the Sower must fit within this existing web of commitments. When a person becomes a monk he deliberately severs all personal ties, so that he can be wholly absorbed in the life of the monastery. In our case we sever no ties on entering the community. But our life together must enhance and strengthen, rather than threaten and weaken, the other communities to which we belong. Everyone at times finds the different commitments pulling them in opposite directions, and making incompatible demands; there is a danger that the community can simply worsen this conflict if we allow our communal activities to expand and multiply. But if our mutual commitment is stable and firm, we can go through long periods of very limited personal involvement, and still derive strength and spiritual energy from one another.

When a person or a married couple is considering whether to join the community, they should be helped to see clearly both the extent and the limits of the commitment they would make. Our rule of life requires us to pray daily, if possible in groups, but otherwise alone or as a couple; to come together each week for Communion and to share a meal with other members; to support one another in our material stewardship and in our various ministries; and to seek always to be at one, forgiving one another's wrongs. The rule thus expresses what we believe are the basic requirements of any Christian community; and a member need do no more within the community than what the rule requires. The question for prospective members is whether such a community is right for them – or whether the greater demands of a monastery, or the more limited common life of the parish church, is more appropriate for their discipleship of Christ.

This balance between the monastic and the parochial pattern of life applies also to the length of our mutual commitment. The monk takes vows that bind him to the monastery for life. The member of a parish church is free to leave it at any time; and those who know they will only be in a place for a few weeks or months are welcomed fully into its worship and fellowship. We formally commit ourselves for a year; but when a person joins he should intend to renew that commitment for several years at least. This stability of membership allows time for that quality of trust to grow which comes from supporting one another through good times and bad times alike; and through such trust the bare skeleton of the rule becomes a living body. Yet members are free to leave at any time if they believe God is calling them to follow Christ elsewhere; and, if the body is strong, it will not only survive the loss of a member, but will be able to bless and support them in their new life.

The community, at any moment in its history, is a particular bunch of people, with their various personalities and temperaments. When someone joins he not only undertakes to follow the rule, but also to share his life with the actual men, women and children who are his fellow members. Before joining he only had quite superficial impressions of them, but over the years he will discover within them both strengths and weaknesses that he could never have imagined beforehand. Thus to enter the community is to share one's spiritual pilgrimage with travelling companions who are virtual strangers; what matters is that they are all travelling in the right direction.

. . . worshipping him together in prayer and in action

During the course of each day we each have different work to do, and go off in different directions. But once a day, for twenty minutes or so, we do the same thing: we pray, saying the same psalms, reading the same passages from the Bible, and praying for the same member of the community. And once a week we share the bread and wine of the Communion.

To a Benedictine monk, accustomed to perhaps eight services a day, worshipping together only once a day may seem rather slack; while to an ordinary parishioner accustomed only to Sunday worship it may appear fearsomely rigorous. But it was the pattern adopted by the first church in Jerusalem which, like our community, contained all sorts and conditions of people; and the apostles must have believed that it was a discipline everyone could follow.

At times all of us will find daily prayer a burden; the service will seem arid and unsatisfying, God will feel remote, and we will be tempted to give up for a period. At others, when the spirit of prayer flows more strongly, we will want more corporate worship. Our common discipline of daily worship sustains us through periods of weakness, since those who are strong in spirit inwardly carry those who are weak. For each of us daily prayer should become a habit, like cleaning one's teeth or combing one's hair in the morning, so deeply ingrained that one does it regardless of mood or feeling.

Praying together – like any shared activity – is an art, requiring skill and sensitivity. It is good to have people taking it in turns to lead services so that no one is always burdened with this responsibility; but equally those who lead should do it sufficiently often that they can be calm and unflustered in their manner, so the service is peaceful and unhurried. When reciting the psalms and the responses together we should each listen as well as speak, so that the tempo and pitch of our voices blend. In our free prayer we should be brief and direct, using our natural speech and tone of voice; long prayers spoken in formal, stilted style soon become wearisome and distracting for others. Although it may at times be tempting to deviate, we should stick strictly to our set form of worship: in this way we can relax, and concentrate not on the service

12

itself but on God. And we should start and finish our worship on time, so that it can fit neatly into our daily routine.

Praying together is usually easier than praying alone. But there will be some members who are not able to pray in a group: they have to leave too early for work; they must look after their small children; or they are too old or sick to leave the house. In the case of a married couple they may try to find a regular time during the day when they can worship together, but for others it may be necessary to worship alone. Our form of daily worship is designed for solitary as well as group use; and the knowledge that, although alone, one is sharing fully in the community's worship is itself a source of strength.

Prayer and action should of course complement each other in our lives. Sincere prayer bears fruit in loving action: if we honestly pray for one another and for the needs of the world, then we shall want to love one another and serve our neighbours. If we listen carefully to God, and he speaks to us both through the Bible and through silence, then our actions shall be wise and sensitive. Likewise if in our daily lives we are peaceful, then we shall be peaceful in our prayers also, wanting to relax in God's presence. But if our lives are rushed and unbalanced, worship – especially in silence – will often seem oppressive, and we may even resent the time spent in prayer. Prayer is not some optional extra to our lives; it is the heart from which the rest of our life should flow.

God binds us together in mutual trust . . .

Committing oneself to community is a single act, made at a particular moment: it is the sowing of a seed. The plant which grows from that seed is trust: people growing in mutual understanding, learning to depend and rely on one another, feeling secure in each other's love. Trust starts to grow at once, but continues to deepen its roots and mature over months, years and decades.

The health of a plant – the quality of trust in the community – cannot readily be measured. But it can be judged by various outward fruits, which are the signs of the community's well-being. The first is quietness. If we trust one another we shall feel relaxed in each other's company: our conversation will flow easily, but we shall be equally happy to work or sit together in silence. If, however, we are insecure with one another, we shall tend to chat interminably and aimlessly, unable to be quiet in each other's presence. Insecurity and lack of trust will also affect our common work: we shall, probably without realising it, be more hurried and anxious in our work, afraid of making mistakes or being judged lazy. But if there is mutual trust we shall feel free to work at our own pace and in our own way – and so be far more efficient and vigorous in what we do.

The second fruit of mutual trust is honesty: people can say what they think and feel without fear of reproach. If we do not feel at ease with one another we shall guard what we say: we shall be wary of causing offence through innocent remarks which are misconstrued; and we shall be anxious to impress others, or at least to say nothing that would lower people's regard for us. And we shall listen to one another with anxious ears, detecting innuendos and insults where none exist. Thus conversation becomes stilted and awkward, and even at times an elaborate game in which we are forced to guess the true thoughts and feelings behind people's words. But if we trust one another we can be honest and straight-forward in what we say. We shall feel free to discuss openly matters of common concern in the community, and also to express our views about wider issues such as politics and theology. At times there will be misunderstandings because words are imperfect vehicles for human thought and feeling; but these can readily be cleared up without any lasting damage being caused. Most important of all, we shall learn more from one another, because, when people feel free to speak their mind, everyone will offer insights and ideas that are fresh and original.

The third and most visible sign of mutual trust is good humour. In an Ethiopian monastery, when the monks gather together for a common meal, their laughter can often be heard echoing round the mountains; and even serious meetings often erupt with irrepressible good humour. So it should be with us. Daily life is full of inconsistencies and ironies, upsets and mishaps, which can engender sullen resentment and irritation. But if we feel secure in each other's love, ill feeling can melt away in laughter: resentment is turned into pleasure, irritation into enjoyment. Humour can, of course, easily be abused, degenerating into sour sarcasm and bitter cynicism. But humour rooted in mutual trust is gentle, preferring paradox to mockery, more ready to laugh at oneself than at others. And its ultimate source is the humour of God, whose purpose in creation is at once both serious and playful.

. . . that we may support one another through warm and tender friendship

People living in ordinary towns and cities often find themselves isolated, with little personal contact with those around them. Old people, and also many young single people, often feel lonely and vulnerable; and families can become inward-looking, with young mothers in particular feeling imprisoned by the home. Many new communities, in reaction to this isolation, go to the opposite extreme, cooking and eating every meal together, sharing the housework and the gardening, and relaxing together in the evenings. Soon people feel themselves oppressed by such close contact, and yearn for solitude and privacy; married couples find the bond between them invisibly weakening, and children feel bewildered and confused.

A community must strike a balance between privacy and sharing, solitude and togetherness. Monasteries, with many centuries of experience, have found various ways of achieving this. In the Benedictine monastery every meal is shared and the monks sleep in dormitories, so physically the monk has no privacy; but for long periods of the day the monks keep silent, so they can find solitude within quietness. In the Pachomian monastery each monk has his own hut where he sleeps and eats alone; the monks meet only once a day for worship, and they eat together usually only once a week and at festivals. Since they live separately there is no need for a strict rule about silence, and often the monks will sit and chat after the day's work is done. Some monks who want more solitude live as hermits in huts near the monastery, coming only for worship.

In our community, which includes families as well as single people, the Pachomian pattern is more appropriate. It is vital that every member has their own private accommodation in which they can cook for themselves, and relax in solitude. A group which includes children cannot observe strict rules of silence; so we must find the quietness we need by being physically separate. Our rule requires us to meet daily for worship, and also to eat with other members of the community once a week. But beyond this each of us must find the degree of sharing that is right for ourselves. Families will usually want to eat alone, while single people may prefer to cook and eat together more often. In our daily work within the community some prefer to work on their own, while others enjoy being in a group. The gregarious members should not cajole others into being more sociable than they would otherwise choose; and more solitary members should not despise the conviviality of others. Rather we should respect one another's freedom, and rejoice in the variety of temperaments and styles of life within the community.

The greatest pleasure of community life is the warm friendships that grow between members. Living in an ordinary town few of us would have chosen one another as friends, because we have such diverse interests and personalities. And when a person first joins the community they may feel quite incapable of being friendly with such a wide assortment of people. Yet over the years, if we have the right balance between solitude and sharing, we each discover a degree of intimacy and tenderness that we could never have imagined.

May we be loyal and steadfast partners in his service . . .

When a monk joins a Benedictine monastery he takes a vow of stability, that he will remain in that community for the rest of his life. Thus the community becomes a family, in which the monks are bound to one another as closely as blood brothers, and the monastery buildings are the family home.

Our promises are made only for a year. But we too need stability: the sense that we are bound to one another through bad times as well as good. In a marriage a couple can have a deep disagreement and a blazing row without ever questioning the marriage bond itself; and this security within the marriage enables them to speak honestly to one another, knowing that in the end any wrong words spoken in anger will be forgiven and forgotten. Within the community we, too, should be able to argue and disagree, even at times to shout at one another in fury, without anyone calling into question our mutual covenant. As in a marriage, once someone starts to use moral blackmail, threatening to leave unless they get their way, the very fabric of the community is threatened: their disagreement becomes a struggle for survival, and honesty gives way to deviousness. If we remain loyal to one another then even the most bitter disagreement, the most furious argument, will be the means to deeper mutual understanding, and hence to stronger love.

In addition to stability of membership we need stability in our pattern of life. There is a temptation within a community constantly to question and alter the routine and organisation, imagining that by tinkering with outward matters our inner problems will be solved. In fact the opposite is true. Frequent change of routine and structure dissipate our energies, cause needless confusions, and undermine our inward sense of security, so that tensions and anxieties multiply. We need to be familiar with the times of the services and meetings so that we barely have to think about them; and we need to know clearly our own responsibilities and those of others, so that practical decisions can be reached easily and quickly. Then we shall be free to concentrate our minds and hearts on the tasks themselves.

A community, like a family, should develop its own traditions and rituals which celebrate its common life. From the outset of our community we have marked people's birthdays. Great effort and imagination is devoted to making a cake whose decoration illustrates some aspect of the person's life: a cake in the shape of a typewriter, perhaps, for the person who does our administrative work; a cake like a henhouse, with toy chickens nearby, for the person who looks after the poultry. At the major festivals of Christmas and Easter we join together for a lunch party, abandoning all normal standards of economy: each household makes some part of the meal, wine flows freely, and afterwards there are wild games for the children and child-like adults. Before lunch on Christmas Day each person receives a present from the community: a few weeks beforehand everyone picks the name of another member out of a hat, and buys them a present under a certain price; these are distributed at Christmas, the names of the donors remaining anonymous – so we each try to guess who chose our present. All these traditions are in themselves trivial and unimportant; but within the context of the community are sacred, symbolising our commitment to one another as a family.

The outsider, looking at the long traditions of monastic life or at our own much newer pattern of life, may imagine that stability breeds stagnation; that a regular rhythm of life will lead to complacency and apathy. But paradoxically the reverse is the case. Stability, rooted in loyalty and faithful commitment to one another, enables us to be flexible and responsive to fresh challenges. If circumstances demand it, any aspect of our pattern of life can be reconsidered; and, afer careful thought, may be altered. And our traditions subtly and gradually evolve, reflecting the changing life of the community. The more secure we are as a community, the greater will be our inner freedom to listen to new ideas and be changed by them.

. . . cherishing one another both in sorrow and in joy

When a boy and girl are simply going out together, enjoying one another's company, they can imagine that sharing the rest of their lives, and loving one another for better or for worse, will be easy. Only when they start living together, sharing practical decisions and responding to each other's anxieties and foibles, do they realise how difficult love can be. Most young couples are surprised at the barriers within themselves that hinder love: petty differences that cause acute irritation; small disagreements that flare up in violent anger; festering resentments at minor injustices; jealousy of each other's freedom; and variations in each other's emotional needs, with one needing more warmth and affection than the other. Both may wonder if their first love was merely an illusion, and they can despair of their marriage. Yet if they stay together, cherishing one another and listening to each other's attitudes and feelings, then the love that emerges is deeper and firmer than they could possibly have imagined during their courtship.

It is the same when people join a community. Beforehand they can imagine it will be easy to love the other members; and those whose previous life was isolated, and are hungry for friendship, will pin high hopes on the new relationships they will make. But as the newcomer settles within the community, meeting other members day by day, then gradually irritations and resentments begin to infect his attitudes. He may want to deny these feelings, to pretend to himself that nothing is amiss. Then he may want to blame the community for the difficulties: that the other members are not sufficiently devout in their faith; or that the community's organisation and pattern of life is not right. Yet if he can remain loyal to the community, for all its faults, then he will eventually start to look within himself for the source of what is wrong; and when this happens he will have begun the true task of community life.

God has called us into community not because we are already saints, able to love everyone who crosses our path, but because we are sinners who need to learn how to love. Before we join most of us vastly underestimate how much we have to learn, imagining ourselves to be warmer and more caring than we really are; and the initial despair is in truth the breaking of that illusion. Yet the illusion is horribly persistent, and often in the future we shall be lulled again into complacent self-esteem; and then some trivial event, some unexpected row or acute sense of jealousy, will jolt us back into reality. But as in a marriage, so in community: whether we feel loving or hateful, good or bad towards one another, we must continue to cherish each other, remaining loyal to our mutual commitment. Only within such a firm, unbreakable bond, will we have the courage to try and deepen our love: to open our hearts to one another, to allow others to see us as we are, to accept others as we find them.

God has made us members one of another with Christ as our head . . .

People are often fearful that, if they belong to a community, they shall be forced to conform to a particular outlook and way of life, and that their individuality and freedom will be lost. Paradoxically people can also be hopeful that community life will satisfy all their emotional needs, that the love and friendship within the community will bring contentment, saving them the need to look outside for friendship.

Both that fear and that hope are false; and we must see clearly their falsehood in order to understand the true nature of community. A monastery, though all the members are the same sex, are single, and typically belong to the same Christian tradition, will still contain a wide range of different temperaments; and so within the framework of a strict rule each member will need a slightly different pattern of life. In this community we not only differ in temperament, but some are single while others are married; there are infants, children and teenagers, as well as adults of all ages; members have a variety of jobs, each making different demands and possibly with different hours of work; and we come from various Christian traditions. The challenge – and the continuing fascination – is to find unity within such diversity, to be brothers and sisters of an extended Christian family without sacrificing our differences. For this reason our rule is very simple, to fit within any way of life: the daily prayer can be said in groups or in individual families as people need; and the only regular commitments beyond this are to come to a weekly communion service, and to share a meal with other members once a week. We must beware of putting further obligations on members, or to imagine that those who have the time and opportunity to be in closer contact with others are superior in their commitment to those who cannot. Any additional requirement is likely to exclude certain types of person; and it is vital that our community can include all sorts and conditions.

The hope that community life will satisfy all our emotional needs is equally dangerous. A monastic community which is enclosed or in the desert may appear to be emotionally self-sufficient; but in truth the monks deliberately accept much greater solitude than is normal, often at the cost of great spiritual anguish, in order to devote themselves emotionally and spiritually more fully to God. Some amongst us may be called to a relatively solitary life, while most need frequent human company and close friendship. Yet if we look only within the community for friendship we shall find ourselves putting heavy emotional burdens on one another; and when others do not respond to our needs, we shall feel bitter and resentful. More importantly, a community that looks only inwards will quickly grow stale and dull, and lose a sense of proportion, with trivial community matters becoming unduly important. We should take trouble to maintain existing friendships outside the community, and make new ones within our neighbourhood, enjoying all types of human company.

The image of community in the New Testament is that of a body, with each member as a different organ. Just as an organ can only remain healthy as part of a body, so human beings need to belong to communities in order to be spiritually healthy; isolated individuals, cut off from others, lose all meaning and purpose in their lives. Yet equally, just as an organ has its own particular role – its own rhythm and way of working – so each member of a community needs his own role and pattern of life to suit his abilities and needs; a community which stifles individual freedom will destroy itself from within. And just as the organs in a body need food and water, so members of a community need the constant spiritual nourishment of friendship and ideas from outside.

. . . that we may be joined together in common vision and purpose

Throughout the history of the Church there has been tension – and at times downright opposition – between the Marthas and the Marys: between those who put greater emphasis on the outward, active side of Christian life, and those who emphasize its inner, spiritual aspects. Often it is merely a matter of personal preference and vocation: some are called to a more active life, and some to a more contemplative one. But sometimes the tension betrays conflicting views of the nature of our faith. Many Christians see prayer and worship as little more than a means of restoring their spiritual energy and moral commitment, in order to engage more effectively in their daily work. For them the object of our faith is to further the kingdom of God in the world through evangelism, charitable works, and social action; and prayer is a means to this end. Others, however, see spiritual growth as the purpose of our faith. For them prayer and worship are central, and the mission of the church is simply to encourage others to share in this inward spiritual journey.

This tension has led to a sharp division amongst the traditional religious communities, between the active and the contemplative orders. In Benedict's time – and indeed to the Ethiopian monk – such a distinction would have been unthinkable. But since the sixteenth century there have been some orders who devote themselves almost entirely to prayer, while others are dedicated to various ministries such as teaching, evangelism or nursing. Since our community is so varied in its membership, we frequently experience this tension within the community itself. There are some amongst us who desire a quiet, well-ordered life in which prayer and contemplation can flourish; and they may resent any disruption. Others want the community to be more energetic and active, helping those in need, supporting various social and political causes, and spreading the gospel; they may despise the apparent apathy of the quieter members.

In truth both are essential aspects of the Christian life; and it is the special vocation of Christian communities to embrace both contemplation and action within a single group of people. Jesus did not specialise in either one or the other: he spent much time in prayer, often going off on his own to spend whole days in quiet contemplation; and also he devoted himself whole-heartedly to preaching the gospel and helping the needy. In today's world prayer and action are of necessity divided for most Christians: prayer takes place at home or in church amongst fellow Christians, while the opportunities to help others and to speak about the gospel are to be found at work or in the local neighbourhood away from church. Thus the connections between the two aspects of Christian life are largely invisible and unspoken. But in a community the connection can be visible and explicit. The same group of people who pray together also work together, and their prayers can find direct expression in their actions.

Within our community it is vital that the inner and outer aspects of our life are held together in a single vision and a single pattern of life. The balance between contemplation and action will vary between members; and each of us will find that the balance within our own life changes as we grow older. But within the community as a whole these variations should not become sources of conflict, but rather be seen as complementary. Our different activities, both inside and outside the community, can be brought together in our daily prayers, so that each of us is supported in spirit by the whole community. And prayer itself is enriched when together we offer the experiences and the struggles of our daily work to God. At times the quiet calm of the community will be interrupted by a person who has come to stay suffering from severe mental and emotional problems; but instead of being irritated at our peace being disrupted, we can embrace that person's needs within our prayers. At other times a member may be exhausted through overwork, and unable to relax; then the steady, unchanging rhythm of the community's daily prayer can bring him inward peace, restoring his spiritual balance.

When George Herbert rebuilt Leighton Bromswold church he installed what appears to be two pulpits, of identical size and height, on either side of the church. In fact only one is a pulpit, and the other is the prayer desk from which the minister leads worship. In his time the Church was divided between Puritans who emphasized preaching the gospel, and High Churchmen who thought prayer was central. For George Herbert each depended on the other: prayer without preaching would become mere spiritual fantasy; and preaching without prayer would be mere intellectual speculation. Each of us has a vocation to preach the gospel, not necessarily in word, but in the quality of our daily work and our attitudes to others; and each of us is called to pray, to contemplate the love and beauty of God.

May we receive graciously into our midst those whom God sends . . .

We do not choose who becomes a member of the community; it is God who sends people. When someone inquires about joining, we should respond openly and warmly, regardless of whether we like them or whether they hold similar views to our own, and we should offer to share with them in trying to discern God's will.

The first step when an individual or family approaches the community is for them to talk to a pastor as to what membership means, and to meet some other members so they can see at first hand the personal implications of belonging. It may take several conversations with a pastor, and several visits to other members, before the newcomer has even an inkling of whether it may be right to join. There should be no hurry, no pressure to reach a decision, but rather we should happily give whatever support and guidance the newcomer needs in considering such a major step in their lives. And it is vital that we should be honest with the newcomer, not trying to impress or persuade, but simply laying before them both the blessings and the difficulties of community life.

Then, when both pastor and newcomer feel it is right, the newcomer joins fully in the life of the community, not yet becoming a full member, but sharing in its worship and fellowship. This step will have different implications for different people. For some, already living near an existing group of community members, it may mean little change: they can remain in the same house, and continue their present job. For others, living away from any group, it may mean moving house and changing job, or alternatively seeking to follow our rule of life in their own situation, hoping that others may join them to form a new group. The greater the change in their pattern of life the prospective member will need to make, the more convinced they should be of the rightness of membership before making concrete steps towards joining. And the pastor, and other members, in giving support and guidance, should think only of what is right for the prospective member, putting aside their own preferences and the needs of the community as a whole.

24

The novice in a monastery may wait many years before taking full vows, after which every aspect of his life is subject to the monastic rule. Our community embraces only part of our lives, and we do not take vows, so the decision to accept full membership can be taken more quickly. Prior to our annual Covenant service, at which our commitment as members is renewed, the pastor should talk to those newcomers who are already sharing the life of the community, and ask whether they want full membership; and the pastor may then commend them at the annual meeting of the community. The decision to accept a new member must be reached with the unanimous consent of the whole community. This does not mean that every existing member should know the newcomers well enough to make their own individual judgement; rather they can trust the judgement of those who are in close contact with the newcomers, and so welcome them whole-heartedly.

Benedict in his Rule warns against accepting into the community those he calls 'wanderers'. These are people who appear sincere in their commitment, but in reality are interested only in the benefits they can derive from the community, and will leave whenever it suits them. Such people are a danger to us too. Some clearly just want to be cared for, and our natural sympathy may tempt us to accept them into membership. But membership implies the willingness to give, as well as to receive, and to share responsibilities; thus although it may be right for us to look after people in need, this should be clearly distinguished from membership. There are others, however, who pose a more profound threat to the community: those who are idealists, full of enthusiasm for our life, but whose real allegiance is not to the community or to the people within it, but to their own ideas. We can easily be flattered by their approval, and imagine that their zeal will breathe fresh life into the community. But once accepted into membership, they will constantly be trying to manipulate the community to turn it into a vehicle for their own vision; and they will be unwilling to listen and to learn from the insights of older members. If we resist such pressure we condemn ourselves to constant dispute and argument; if we give way, we endanger our very existence.

Receiving new members – and the desire of new people to join – is a visible affirmation of the community's well-being. There are also times when it is right for an existing member to leave; and if they depart in love and peace, that too is a sign of the community's strength. A member may decide that having been led by God to join the community, God is now calling him to a new path; and the other members, despite the sadness of parting, should encourage and bless his move. There may also be times when the community must consider withdrawing a person's membership. This should never occur because of personal dislike, or because the individual is awkward or difficult, but only when he is unwilling to abide by the community's rule of life, either in letter or in spirit. Someone who has drifted away from the worship and fellowship of the community, or who is out of harmony with the spirit of the community, should be asked by a pastor to look afresh at the pattern and direction of his life. The person may decide to renew his commitment, or to leave freely; but if he refuses either alternative, the pastor must bring the matter to the whole community for its decision. Whatever the outcome, even if at worst a person is expelled from membership, the community should continue to offer love and friendship.

. . . growing as one body in his love

Over the centuries people have commonly asked of monasteries: what are they for, what purpose do they serve? And monks are often accused of escaping from the world, of opting out of the task of creating a better society. The same questions and accusations are frequently put to us. And we may be tempted to offer some outward purpose, such as welcoming guests or caring for people in need, as the justification for our existence.

Yet people never ask these questions of marriage: married life is not expected to justify itself by some outward service to society. Marriage exists for its own sake, and is considered a good and desirable way of life. Indeed the Church has often seen married love as a symbol of heaven, where the union of hearts and bodies is perfect. A good marriage will often bear outward fruits: through their mutual support husband and wife can often work and serve others more effectively, and their family home can be a place of welcome. But the love that grows and deepens between husband and wife is itself the ultimate purpose of marriage. So it is with us. Christian communities, be they monasteries, lay communities such as ours, or parish churches, exist for their own sake. They are places where people are brought together, in worship and fellowship, to learn to love God and love one another. Such communities will always bear outward fruits: they will be places where strangers feel welcome; they will offer hope to the lonely and vision to the bewildered; and their common prayer will be powerful in the service of others. But these are the consequences, not the purpose, of us coming together in unity.

Those who have lived in a close-knit community know that it is not an escape. The secular world, with its array of entertainments and its insatiable quest for wealth, offers innumerable escape routes from the source of humanity's problems, which is within the human spirit. But in a community, as in marriage, there is no escape: we are forced to confront and attack those inner barriers which prevent us truly giving ourselves in love to others. And nor do members of a community opt out of the task of creating a better society. The secular world measures its progress by economic growth; we bear witness to another, more vital measure of progress, the growth of the human spirit in love and knowledge of God.

As a child grows up year by year he changes in size and shape, in outlook and personality. In the same way our community, if it is to grow in spirit, must constantly be open to change. The newcomer, especially one who possesses clear vision and insight, will often be felt as a threat by existing members, because they sense he will challenge their attitudes and pattern of life. We should welcome such a challenge, encouraging new members to express freely their ideas and insights, so that through them we can look afresh at ourselves. We should also allow our roles within the community to be changed to make way for the gifts of newcomers, and to develop our own gifts in new ways. In the Pachomian monastery it is a mark of pride that younger members are put in positions of responsibility, managing the affairs of the community, while older members can devote themselves more fully to prayer; in this way the community remains fresh and vigorous even over many centuries.

Community is a child that should continue growing up, and never imagine it has reached adulthood. We should enjoy our life together as it is now, rejoicing in the particular gifts and pattern of life we have at present. But we should also live in hope for what we may become, our hearts and minds always open to new people and new visions.

STEWARDSHIP

As God in Christ teaches his people to be faithful stewards of his creation, we pray that through our work and fellowship we may bear a rich harvest of love.

We offer all that we have to be used in his service, asking that we may each receive according to our needs.

God has called us into a loving family of faith, that we may find joy in sharing his rich blessings.

May we be compassionate and sensitive to the needs of others, devoting ourselves with cheerful and willing hearts to the good of all.

God provides us each with many gifts, that we may be generous in our mutual care.

May we be honest and thoughtful in using our talents and resources, performing with diligence the tasks given to us.

As God in Christ teaches his people to be faithful stewards of his creation . . .

In the Jerusalem church the members pooled all their possessions, handing them over to the apostles who distributed them according to need. Like those first Christians, all of us should regard our material wealth and our talents as belonging to God, to be used for the common good. And, like them, we should be totally honest in assessing our wealth and abilities; if we underestimate our resources, in order to reduce the demands on us, we are committing the sin of Ananias and Sapphira who deceived the apostles.

Yet the actual system of stewardship must vary according to circumstances. The total communism of the Jerusalem church requires detailed central management, assessing people's needs and also directing people's work. As the Jerusalem church grew in numbers the apostles found themselves unable to perform this task, and people started to grumble at their inefficiency. And although seven managers were appointed to assist, it seems that the experiment was short-lived. In the churches founded by Paul there was no pooling of wealth. Each household remained materially independent, but was expected to give part of its income to the church, especially in response to appeals to help needy churches elsewhere. Thus Paul's churches operated much like a modern parish church.

The monasteries revived the communism of Jerusalem. In reaction against the wealth the Church was accumulating, they committed themselves to poverty in which the individual monk owned nothing. Since there were no families to support, and the monks desired only the basic necessities, the management of the monastery remained simple. Some centuries later Francis of Assisi, whose way of life was like that of the early monks, was asked how his ideals could be applied to ordinary families. In response he wrote a special rule for families, and founded an order, later known as the Third Order. In this each family remains responsible for its own wealth, but must talk regularly with a spiritual director as to how best to use its talents and resources in the service of God.

For Nicholas Ferrar and George Herbert there was no need to create a new system of stewardship, since the communities they created were based on their own families. But for the lay communities founded from the early twentieth century onwards the use of wealth has proved a major stumbling block. Many have tried to imitate the communism of Jerusalem and the monasteries. But this means setting up a central authority over the families, so that the community, rather than the parents, has ultimate charge of the children. And since families' needs and abilities vary greatly, the task of management becomes unbearably complex. Sooner or later people reassert their freedom, and the community breaks apart.

The pattern we have adopted is that of Francis's Third Order. Each of us remains independent, deciding what work to do, and how to allocate our income and wealth. But every year we must make a detailed assessment of our stewardship, reviewing every aspect of our use of time and money. We each have a confidential meeting with a pastor to whom we present our assessment; he in turn asks questions and offers advice to ensure we have been both honest and just in our stewardship of God's gifts. At any time in the course of the year when we have an important decision to take affecting our stewardship – such as changing job, or moving house – then again we must seek the advice of a pastor. In talking to a pastor we are compelled to look clearly at our actions, so that our inner conviction that everything belongs to God bears fruit in our outward lives.

. . . we pray that through our work and fellowship we may bear a rich harvest of love

Benedict taught that the tools of the monastery – the spades and ploughs, the pots and pans – are as sacred as the vessels on the altar. For him the material and the spiritual aspects of community life are of equal importance since it is through working and eating together, and through sharing practical decisions, that we grow together in spirit. Similarly Nicholas Ferrar, in establishing the community at Little Gidding, gave as much importance to the work and the social life of the members as to their worship. The three acts of worship each day – Matins, the Litany and Evensong – were immediately followed by the three main meals. And, according to the gifts of the members, various enterprises were set up: a workshop for bookbinding, and another for tapestry weaving; a herb garden and a dispensary in which herbal remedies were made and given out to local people; a school for their own and local children; and alms houses in which elderly people were looked after. Nicholas's nieces also started a study circle, known as the Little Academy, in which they related and discussed stories from history and classical mythology.

The loneliness that many people suffer in our society stems from the material isolation of their lives. At work they may be in an office or factory in which there is little sharing of decisions or mutual support. And at home families are economically independent, self-contained within their own houses, so that social contact is often no more than polite conversations in the street. In joining a community people are breaking out of this isolation, and seeking a physical and material context in which human love can flourish naturally. Thus, like Benedict and Nicholas Ferrar, we must recognise that our pattern of work and fellowship is as vital to our spiritual well-being as the pattern of prayer and worship.

In the Benedictine monastery the monks are in each other's company throughout the day and night: they not only eat every meal together, but sleep in large dormitories. In the Pachomian monastery, by contrast, monks live in their own huts where they sleep and eat, coming together only once a week for a common meal; but they work together day by day in the fields, repairing the buildings, and running the monastery school. In a community of families such as ours the Pachomian pattern is more appropriate. The family itself is the basic community, and needs its own house in which meals are shared and the family relaxes together. Our regular social contact is limited to only one meal a week, although many choose to eat together or drop into each other's homes for a drink more often. But, as in a Pachomian monastery, it is through our common work that we are drawn together more closely. There are the basic tasks of cleaning and maintaining the community buildings, and also looking after the elderly and sick members of the community. In addition, as members' gifts and time allow, we join together in other enterprises: a small farm in which we rear animals and grow fruit and vegetables for our own consumption; a printing and publishing firm; a hostel for young people; a herb garden and workshop in which the herbs are processed and packed for sale. None of these ventures are in themselves intrinsic to the life of the community; and new ventures may start, and old ones stop, as new members join and old members retire or move on. But they are the sacraments of our life as a community: the outward and visible activities which bind us together inwardly as brothers and sisters.

We offer all that we have to be used in his service . . .

There are two illusions about stewardship to which most of us are prone. The first is to value wrongly our gifts and talents. A few proud people over-estimate their gifts, but most vastly under-estimate them. This is not simply out of modesty or humility, but also from fear and selfishness, because to recognise fully the gifts God has bestowed is to accept responsibility for using them for the common good. The second illusion is to imagine that we are using our money and material wealth in a frugal, economical manner: we will admit to only a few minor extravagances, but otherwise think of ourselves as living quite simply. In truth most of us enjoy material privilege far above the majority of humanity, and waste money on trivial and unnecessary goods; but to acknowledge this is to accept far greater responsibility for the needs of the poor.

The purpose of our annual review of stewardship is to compel us to look honestly at our gifts and talents, our income and wealth; and so take full responsibility as to how we use them.

The first stage of the review is for the community as a whole to make a budget for its own expenditure in the coming year, so that members know what their contributions must be. For those living in houses owned by the community we must set a rent based on all the costs incurred. But in addition to this the community has a central fund to which every member contributes, regardless of where they live. This fund is used partly for central community buildings, but also to finance community ventures, and to support particular members in their ministry to the wider church. The extent to which we can undertake new projects or support members' work depends entirely on the contributions of members. Members are free to decide, as part of their own stewardship, how much they should contribute to the central fund. Thus when we draw up the budget, we are setting ourselves a target at which to aim.

Once the community budget is complete we each begin our own personal review of stewardship, scrutinising carefully our use of both time and money. There is no single method for undertaking this review since people's gifts and material circumstances vary widely, and their ways of thinking are so different. But for most of us it is helpful to look at a typical week, mapping out – perhaps on paper – how our time is spent. The conclusions may be quite shocking, smashing cherished illusions about ourselves: we may be horrified at how little time is spent in prayer and meditation, and even less in serious study and reflection on our faith; and how much time seems to be frittered away in useless and unsatisfying leisure, which refreshes neither body nor spirit. Then we should set down a simple account of our income and expenditure; and again the results may surprise us. Our income may be far in excess of that of the poor and unemployed in society, yet we may give away only a tiny fraction of what we receive, dissipating large amounts on trivial goods and activities which we neither need nor enjoy. Once we have looked with brutal honesty at our present situation, then we must ask how we can improve matters. We could question whether we could use our gifts more fully in the service of others; how the pattern of our life could be changed to devote not only more time but also more energy to prayer and reflection; and how our income could be used more fruitfully, so that we ourselves derive more enjoyment and also have more to give away.

When we have drawn up our own personal assessment, each individual and married couple then meets in confidence with a pastor of the community to discuss it. Although the pastor is an ordinary member of the community – and indeed the pastors themselves must undertake the same review of stewardship – at these meetings he represents God to us: in presenting our decisions to him, clearly and honestly, we are acknowledging that we are answerable to God for how we use our talents and resources. Thus, just as God never overrules us but always upholds our freedom, so the pastor's task is not to compel or cajole us towards particular decisions, but rather to support us in seeking the right decisions for ourselves. He should listen carefully, asking questions so he understands fully our thoughts and attitudes. Once he has seen the whole picture, then he should offer advice as he feels appropriate, suggesting changes we may make; and we for our part should have the courage to ask advice, remembering that we remain free to accept or reject it as we see fit. Most important of all, he should encourage us to look more deeply at our own gifts and abilities, helping us to discover talents that lie hidden within us, and affirming us in spheres where we remain timid and uncertain of our own capacities.

The pastors should take note of what people intend to contribute in the coming year to the community's central fund. Then once the stewardship meetings are complete these figures should be added up, and compared to the budget. If the contributions are as high as we had planned, then the pastors can report this to the community without need for further discussion. But if the contributions are not enough, then we must either reduce our planned expenditure – and so curtail part of our ministry – or ask ourselves to look again at our personal stewardship. There should be no moral pressure on members to raise their contributions. Rather each of us should weigh up the various demands on our income, and, after thought and prayer, make our own decision. We must trust that God is speaking to the community through the financial contributions of its members: if the figure is too small we should be ready to look again at our plans, questioning whether they are right; and if the contributions are sufficient we can go forward in confidence.

. . . asking that we may each receive according to our needs

Benedict taught that the monk's life should be balanced: there should be balance between work and leisure, between mental and manual activities, and between material comfort and simplicity. Only if there is balance in these outward aspects of life will prayer flow freely and naturally. For us, faced with the demands of family life and of earning a living in the world, such a balance is far harder to achieve; yet it is equally vital for both our spiritual and physical health.

Some of us are tempted to work excessively, perhaps out of fear of stillness, or out of an obsessive desire to prove our abilities; every task is treated as urgent, and life is a frenzied rush from one activity to the next. Others amongst us are tempted in the opposite direction towards idleness, perhaps out of apathy and lack of purpose in our lives, or because small emotional upsets absorb excessive amounts of energy. The Benedictine monastery can impose a healthy balance between work and recreation through the strictness of its daily routine; we, however, must each find the right routine for ourselves. In our annual review of stewardship we should look carefully at the typical pattern of each day and week, and be willing if necessary to make radical changes to ensure we are neither burning ourselves out or dissipating our abilities.

In modern society, with its sharp division of labour, the right balance between mental and manual work can be even harder to achieve. Most jobs are so specialised that they use only a narrow range of our capacities: so while some spend the entire day in concentrated mental effort, others do only physical work. Yet community life can, to some degree, redress this balance. At the very least it can provide opportunities for different kinds of work for people to do at weekends or in the evenings. The person whose job is purely mental can dig potatoes or milk cows on the community's farm, or help repair and decorate the community's buildings. And the person whose employment is mainly manual can share in administrative tasks or write sermons for the weekly communion services. More fundamentally the community can enable some to shift from full-time to part-time employment by providing gainful work in the community itself: if our community ventures operate efficiently, either providing for our own needs directly or selling goods which others buy, then members can find a more varied and balanced pattern by working partly outside and partly within the community.

The balance between simplicity and comfort is impossible to strike satisfactorily, and we inevitably find ourselves making uneasy compromises. In a world where millions are near to starvation, the call of justice is to give all we can to help them. Yet equally we must ensure our own children are healthy, and have the toys, books, education and outside activities to develop their own faculties to the full. And we ourselves need not only good food, but also a comfortable home if we are to have the physical and psychological strength to work to the best of our abilities. There is no way to reconcile our own material needs with those of others, and we must accept that an unjust world imposes a permanent moral conflict on all of us. Rather we must constantly ask how we can simplify our lives, reducing our own use of the world's resources in order to have more to give to others.

The fruit of a balanced life is holiness, not in the sense of being unusually pious or devout, but of being healthy physically, emotionally and spiritually. And this in turn enables us to love and serve God, and our fellows, to the full extent of our natural abilities. If we are constantly rushing from one task to another, and are mentally exhausted, then we shall have no time or energy to give ourselves in love. As we talk with others we shall be looking at the clock, rather than listening to what they are saying; and prayer itself will seem an awkward intrusion into a busy schedule. Similarly if we are lazy, spending too much of the day chatting idly or amusing ourselves with light magazines and television programmes, then friendship will become dull, and quite small jobs will seem too hard; and we shall constantly be looking for excuses to avoid prayer. But if the balance of our life is right, then we shall have ample time and energy for God and for other people.

God has called us into a loving family of faith . . .

In most respects monastic communities, and communities such as ours, face the same challenges in achieving a balanced and healthy pattern of life. But there is one challenge we face which monasteries do not share: to find the right balance between the family and the community. The original community at Little Gidding avoided this problem because it was based on a single extended family, the Ferrars. We, by contrast, are a group of separate families, with no ties of blood, and with quite diverse backgrounds. Many communities of families have foundered because the demands of the community have overwhelmed family life; and families have only been able to survive by leaving the community. Yet if the balance is right the opposite will occur: the isolation many families experience within modern society will be overcome, and family life will be enriched and enhanced by the community.

The balance between family and community needs to be struck at three levels. The first is in the use of money and other material resources. If money and resources are pooled then decisions about what food to eat, what clothes to wear, where to go on holiday, what toys to buy, and all the other economic decisions we have to make, must be made by the community rather than the family. Thus parents find themselves applying to the community for their needs. And also decisions about what work people do will have to be made by the community, since it is the community's income, not that of the individual family, which is affected by a change in a person's employment. Parents soon feel undermined by the community since their natural desire to care for their children and to provide for their needs is frustrated by the superior will of the community. And children, too, are confused since it is unclear whether their parents or the community have responsibility for their well-being. Thus it is vital that families remain materially independent, and are responsible for the care and upbringing of their children; and that the family decides freely what to spend and what work to do.

The second balance that must be struck is in the use of time. For a husband and wife already too busy, with too little time to spend together, the community can easily be yet another demand on their time, taking them away from each other. And a couple whose marriage is already weak and unhappy may, without deliberate intention, use the life of the community as a way of avoiding one another. Yet, if the other pressures can be adjusted so there is ample time for both family and community, the community can strengthen even weak marriages. Most outside activities in the modern world take husband and wife in separate directions: their jobs; the clubs and societies to which they belong; even their different circles of friends. But involvement in the community is something they share: it is the same group of people that become their friends; it is the same pattern of prayer and fellowship in which they participate. And their children, too, share the life of the community, often adopting other adult members as aunts and uncles. Thus the common commitment draws the family closer together.

The third, and least visible, balance is within the heart. Even the strongest marriage is not immune from the possibility of the husband or wife forming emotional attachments outside the marriage which, while at first may be harmless, can soon conflict with the emotional and sexual bonds of the marriage itself. Yet close friendships outside the marriage, even with members of the opposite sex, can often fulfil emotional needs which are not met within the marriage; thus the mutual frustration and disappointment that can poison married life may be assuaged. It is vital that the sexual discipline of marriage is maintained rigidly within the community, for even a suspicion of adultery can destroy mutual trust; and it is equally important that the less tangible emotional discipline is maintained, that husband and wife regard their relationship as central to their lives. Within such discipline healthy, loving friendships can flourish, and deep attachments can form, to the benefit both of the community and of the marriages within it. Couples will be able to appreciate what they do provide for one another, without resenting the inevitable limitations of their relationship.

The balance between a family and the community should be embodied in our living arrangements. Each family – and also each single person – should have their own separate house or flat, with a kitchen in which they can cook for themselves, and a front door which defines their area of privacy. On the other hand we should live sufficiently close to one another that everyone in the community is within easy walking distance of other members. At Little Gidding the houses are built around a courtyard, so there is both separation and closeness. Elsewhere, such as at Leighton Bromswold, where members live within a village or town, it is good that their homes should be within a few hundred yards of each other. Not only will this enable them to meet daily for prayer, but also they can readily drop in on one another and help each other with practical tasks.

. . . that we may find joy in sharing his rich blessings

Benedict described his monastery as a school in God's service. Its regular rhythm of prayer, manual work and study was wholly directed to learning the love of God. By a similar comparison our community is a kindergarten. While older children at school follow a set pattern of work, we are young children who play and learn each in our own way and at our own pace, being brought together only at certain times for common activities. So we each have different work to do, some going out to jobs, others looking after children at home; we have different interests, and live in a variety of different situations. And amidst the diversity we come together each day and each week for worship and fellowship. Nonetheless our purpose is the same as that of the monastery: our common life is directed to the love and knowledge of God.

If a school – and to a more limited extent a kindergarten – is to function successfully, it needs a timetable by which the children must abide strictly. If even quite a small number arrive late for lessons, it disrupts the whole school, since lessons must either be delayed or disturbed by the latecomers; and soon those who are punctual decide there is no point in coming on time. The same is true of us: punctuality, an apparently trivial matter, is, as Benedict taught, vital to the happiness of a religious community. The latecomers do not realise the damage they do, since it is the rest who are disrupted. And if a person is persistently late for common worship or meals, for no good reason, it is felt by the rest to show lack of care and respect for the life of the community, and so weakens our common spirit. There are few who are able to time their arrival precisely, so the only way to be sure of being punctual is to aim to arrive early.

Even more important to the life of a school – and a community – is courtesy and good manners which, like punctuality, are often wrongly regarded as trivial. Rudeness, like lateness, quickly affects the whole community. Courtesy consists not primarily in outward observance, but in inward self-control. Adults, like children, are prone to indulge their moods; if a person is seen angry or depressed, these feelings are liable to show themselves in some curt remark or sullen dismissal. And we soon find we are reinforcing each other's negative emotions. Yet even in the blackest moods all of us can, if we are firm with ourselves, afford a friendly greeting and a smile when we meet. And at common meals, even if we're too tired or unhappy to stimulate conversation, we can respond with interest to what others are saying. In a community, as in a school, bad manners can become so commonplace that they are barely noticed, and yet corrode the bonds which hold us together. Conversely, simple acts of courtesy are the most easy and costless way of affirming our care and appreciation of one another, and so strengthen our common bonds.

Benedict recognised that to the outsider becoming a pupil in his school would seem daunting, that the monks' timetable of prayer and work would seem impossibly rigorous for the normal person. But he assures the readers of his Rule that, while the monastic life may seem difficult at first, there is nothing too hard to bear; and that once a person is accustomed to the pattern, it is sweet and joyful. Our much less rigorous kindergarten can also seem daunting to the outsider; and indeed it can take a newcomer a few months to grow used to our simple pattern of common prayer and meetings. Yet if the routine is strictly observed, it becomes a matter of habit, carried on without effort. And if we are gentle and courteous to one another, then our common life, like that of the monastery, is a source of sweetness and joy – making the rest of our daily lives seem much lighter and more pleasant.

May we be compassionate and sensitive to the needs of others . . .

George Herbert advises the country parson to be constantly observant of his parishioners: to visit them in their homes, to discover how each person lives, and to listen with care to their needs and feelings. Only if the help and advice he gives stems from a true understanding of his people will he support their efforts rather than undermine them.

In our community it is not just the leaders, but all of us, who should try to be observant. If we fail to understand each other's true needs, then even our best intentions will be fruitless. The person who is convinced he knows what is right for other people, and sets about providing it, will trample on their self-confidence and destroy their own attempts to do what is right. Even an offer of help which is made too forcefully – and so brooks no refusal – can be felt as hostile and arrogant. Before any of us is qualified to help others, he must first learn to hear the feelings and needs that lie behind people's words and actions; our own spirit must echo to theirs, and so their needs become ours. Then we shall know instinctively the kind of help which will support and strengthen others; and we will avoid pushing people down even as we are trying to pull them up.

The sphere in which this sensitivity is most important is in supporting one another as parents: here the difference between true support, and the kind of help which is in fact a hindrance, is most marked. Every parent wants to do the best for their children, yet all parents at times feel uncertain about their abilities. Inevitably within the community families will have different methods of looking after their children and different standards of discipline. So there is always the temptation for a parent to be critical of other parents, as a way of justifying their own approach; or conversely to feel inadequate in relation to the apparent competence of other parents. Yet the community can provide enormous support to parents, and lighten the responsibility of raising children. There are simple practical actions such as giving parents a rest by taking their children out. But no less important is encouragement, remarking with pleasure on the achievements of children, and helping parents find patience in the face of apparent failures. The community can become an extended family – a family of families – in which the care and love of children is shared. We should never pass moral judgement on parents, or try to persuade them to some other approach to the upbringing of their children; rather we should support them in the approach they have freely decided, and uphold whatever standards of discipline they have set.

Offering help to one another, with care and sensitivity, is an art which all of us can learn with comparative ease; but far more difficult is to ask for and receive help when we need it. Pride and fear, the two greatest barriers to love, stand in the way of turning to others for support: pride makes us imagine ourselves independent, strong and capable enough to fend for ourselves; and fear makes us dread that any request for help will meet with contempt. And so either we refuse to turn to others, or we use devious means to obtain what we want: expressions of self-pity to induce guilt in others, or veiled threats to compel people to give what we desire. Yet in reality the straightforward request for help is almost never treated with contempt, and brings no loss of respect. On the contrary people are pleased at the opportunity to do something of value for others, and they admire the humility of a person who asks. And so each of us must learn to be confident in asking for help, and joyful in receiving it.

. . . devoting ourselves with cheerful and willing hearts to the good of all

The new monk at the Pachomian monastery is given the humblest and most menial tasks – scrubbing floors, digging ditches, and serving meals. This is true not only of young men, but also older men joining the monastery, who perhaps have previously been businessmen, civil servants, teachers or even parish priests. The same is true in Benedictine monasteries: Benedict mentions especially that priests should have no privileges because of their office, but should be treated like the rest. The purpose is for the newcomer to learn humility, through learning how to enjoy even the most lowly task; only then can he be entrusted with greater authority.

In our less rigorous community such a harsh introduction for the newcomer is inappropriate; yet the same spirit is equally important. However grand and important a person's outside job may be, whatever their social background, and whatever position a person may hold in their church, within the community we are all of equal status. And, whatever else we do for the community, all of us who are physically capable should share in the menial tasks that community life involves: cleaning the community dining room and the chapel; helping to prepare meals, and washing up the dishes afterwards; and decorating and maintaining the buildings owned and used by the community.

These tasks can, if done in the right spirit, become acts of worship – and are often more enjoyable, and even hilarious, than any formal acts of worship in the chapel. Standing together at a kitchen sink, or decorating a room together, can be as profound an act of communion as a sharing of the bread and wine at the Lord's Supper. And these shared manual tasks can be a more effective antidote to pride, and a means to humility, than direct prayer or spiritual counsel. Mistakenly we often imagine that to defeat selfish pride we must suppress it, and are then disappointed at its constant resurgence. But it is rather a question of transforming selfish pride into corporate pride, so the pleasure once found purely in one's own achievements becomes pleasure in what we do together. When one feels greater pride in the community's well-being than in one's own personal status – when promotion at work gives less pleasure than the achievements of the community – then the war against pride is being waged successfully.

God provides us each with many gifts . . .

Children, at some stage in their development, begin to display a strong sense of personal ambition, often so fierce as to shock their parents: one child desperately wants to gain a medal in swimming or some other sport; another child can think of little else but learning how to programme a computer; and so on. Although his ambition may involve outstripping his rivals, the child's main desire is to use his gifts and talents to the full. Such ambition is natural, and continues into adulthood; but invariably, as we grow up, our natural ambition is to some degree distorted. The hardest – and most profound – task of Christian stewardship is to direct our natural ambition towards the service of God and our fellows.

Natural ambition is distorted in two ways. The most obvious is that the desire to use our gifts to the full becomes the vehicle for personal advancement and greed. In seeking a career young people are encouraged to use their gifts to acquire the highest income; and a greedy person whose talents have made him wealthy is admired and envied by others. Within a particular group of people – not least within Christian churches and communities – ambition is more often directed towards status and power: people jockey for promotion and preferment, not primarily to serve others more effectively, but because they desire the highest place. And ambition paradoxically can turn into the reverse image of itself, when people come to accept – even desire – failure. There are many for whom the pursuit of ambition has so often been frustrated by the rival ambitions of others that they have given up trying to use their own talents to the full. To remain at the bottom, avoiding the attention of others, comes to feel safe and comfortable.

But, although selfish ambition is so prevalent in our society, it rarely appears naked; rather it disguises itself under a cloak of virtue and respectability. Those whose talents are directed towards acquiring wealth will hardly ever admit their greed, even to themselves, and will often pretend that their material standard of living is no more than the average. Those who desire status will assert their modesty, while those hungry for power will speak only of using their position to serve others. The people who find safety in failure – in burying their talents – will often imagine that their wounded pride is humility.

At our annual review of stewardship, in addition to looking outwards at our use of time and money, we must also look inwards at our attitudes to our gifts and talents. Our talents are given by, and belong to God: so it is our duty to him, as well as to ourselves, to assess them honestly, without false modesty; and then to decide, carefully and rationally, how best to use them in his service. We should not be afraid or ashamed of our ambition to develop our gifts to the full; rather, by directing our ambition towards God, it can become a source of energy and inspiration. We should desire to be fit and healthy – physically, mentally and emotionally – and seek to educate and train our talents in order to realise their fullest potential. And, if we are constantly thankful to God as the source of our talents, then we can take a childlike pride in our achievements.

. . . that we may be generous in our mutual care

Children sometimes show quite extraordinary generosity: they give a much-loved toy to another child who desperately wants it; they give their entire pocket money away to a charity after they've seen an appeal on television. Their parents are taken by surprise, not just because it is unusual, but because they themselves would never act in such a way: adults are too concerned for justice and fairness, and so count the cost of what they give rather than respond spontaneously to another's need. Indeed parents often disapprove of their children's generosity, urging them not to be so reckless.

In a monastery – as in the Jerusalem church – justice and generosity come together in a single act when a new member hands over all his wealth to the community: it is a reckless act of generosity, which enables the members to live as equals, each receiving from the community what they need. For families living in the world this simple approach is impossible: perfect justice cannot be achieved through individual generosity, and a family which responded to every call on its resources would become destitute. Yet even in more limited spheres amongst our friends, our neighbours or even our church, the childlike impulse to be generous is so often thwarted by an obsession with fairness. We hate the thought of being exploited by giving more than our fair share; and so we prefer to be mean with our time and money.

Within our community we do not try to achieve perfect justice, but depend entirely on the generosity of our members. Since each family and single person is materially independent, the community itself cannot impose standards of fairness and equality. Instead we depend on individual members helping others who are in particular need, giving freely their time and money. Thus if an elderly person cannot afford a good holiday, or someone in a lowly-paid job needs a new car but does not have enough money, then the richer members should respond – without fuss, and without telling others what they are doing – by giving money. If a family needs their house to be redecorated, or heavy furniture to be moved, or if a mother needs someone to look after her child while she goes out, then we can offer our time. We should never keep a tally, even in our minds, of how much time and money we've given and received; rather we should give freely, and expect to receive help from others when we need it. The central fund of the community, supporting our mission, also depends on the generosity of our members: people freely decide what to give, and the amount remains confidential so that no one is under moral pressure.

In addition to material generosity, there is another, less tangible, form of generosity which is equally important and can often be more costly: generosity of praise. One can be generous with material things, and yet still be mean-spirited in one's appreciation of the endeavours of others. This meanness may stem from not wanting to acknowledge the superiority of others in certain fields – and hence its root is pride. Or more often it may come from being too absorbed in one's own efforts to spare thought for the achievements of others – and so its root is selfishness. Thus honest and full-hearted praise is an act of spiritual generosity, which sometimes involves profound inward sacrifice.

May we be honest and thoughtful in using our talents and resources . . .

For the ordinary peasant in past centuries who joined a monastery, much of his daily work as a monk was the same as he had done at home. In his village he would have learnt a wide range of skills – agriculture, animal husbandry, building, making simple utensils, and so on; and he would continue these tasks in the monastic community. In one respect, however, he might widen his range of activities: he might be taught to read, and thence to study. An educated man joining the monastery would also widen his range of skills, but from the opposite direction: he would already be able to read and be well versed in theology, but in the monastery he would learn manual skills.

In our society most people are compelled to do highly specialised jobs, and the range of skills needed in daily life is very narrow. For many this is frustrating and unfulfilling, and they waste many natural talents they possess in other spheres. Community life provides an opportunity to broaden our range of activities and to share our skills. A person whose education has been almost entirely intellectual can learn to cook, grow vegetables, dig ditches and lay drains, repair and maintain buildings, and even to arrange flowers in the chapel. And a person whose work has been mainly manual can learn to preach a sermon, lead a service, keep accounts, and manage some department of the community. In our annual review of stewardship we should reflect on whether we are making the broadest use of our talents, or whether there are new skills we could learn in the service of others. And we should be willing to invest in our talents: just as the Ferrar community at Little Gidding, when some of the women wanted to learn book-binding, paid a book-binder to come and teach them, so we should be willing to seek outside training to gain new skills.

Yet, despite the opportunities community life can offer, we still remain in the world, and need to earn money; and the work which is best rewarded financially is unlikely to make the widest use of our talents. Each family within the community is responsible, as far as it is able, to earn enough money for its own needs. Yet if some feel called to contribute in large measure to our community fund, this may enable us to give financial support to particular families to work on behalf of the community. Thus for each family there is a difficult decision as to how to allocate their time between earning money and engaging in work that is of intrinsic value. And, contrary to the values of the world, the desire to earn more money may arise not from greed but from generosity, wanting to support the work and ministry of others in the community.

The more fully people develop and use their talents, the more urgent will become the challenge which every community must face: of whether the richer and more talented members enjoy more power in the community, or whether we can remain truly equal. There is no denying that our natural endowments and talents differ, some people being far more gifted than others; and our financial endowments differ also, since some can earn more money than others, and hence contribute more to the community. In the world power and influence accrue to those who are wealthy and able; and, since we have all imbued the values of the world, this will tend to happen in the community also. We must resist it firmly, sharing power and influence amongst all members equally, allowing people's views and attitudes on each issue to be weighed on their own merit. It is here that our commitment to Christian stewardship is most severely tested, since the only way to ensure true sharing of power is through the sharing of abilities and resources, regarding nothing as belonging to individuals and all as belonging to God.

. . . performing with diligence the tasks given to us

Visitors to Little Gidding church during Nicholas Ferrar's time were astonished at the care that was lavished on it. The community made exquisite tapestries and cushion covers to decorate the church, and each day fresh flowers and herbs were placed there so that it both looked and smelt delicious. The house in which the community lived was more austere in decor, but it too was spotlessly clean. George Herbert, in his guide for the Country Parson, says that one of the priest's first duties is the care of his church, to keep it in good repair, to furnish and decorate it beautifully, and to ensure it is swept perfectly clean. The parson's house should be similarly looked after, and the food at his table should be simple but wholesome, and, where possible, consisting of vegetables grown in his own garden.

The visitor coming to our community will also gain his first impression of us by the cleanliness of our buildings, the care given to their furnishing and decoration, and also by the simplicity and quality of the food we serve. And such an impression, far from being superficial, is justified, because these outward things are signs of the inner quality of our life together. A family rightly wants its home to be clean and pleasant, and will spend great care over furniture and decoration, because these material things are expressions of its family life. In the same way the communal rooms within a community – the chapel and the meeting rooms – are its home, and their decor should express its spirit. There is no need for lavish expense, and we should avoid accumulating unnecessary pieces of furniture and decorative objects to place on mantlepieces or hang on walls – they only make for more cleaning, and are bound to offend the tastes of some members. Rather we should have plain, sturdy furniture, and simple decoration that is easy to clean and maintain. So too with our common meals. Elaborate, costly dishes should be reserved only for special celebrations, such as the baptism of a child or an eightieth birthday party. Our normal weekly common meals should be simple and wholesome, with only a few dishes, so the food can be easily prepared and served.

Rooms that are simple to clean, and food that is simple to cook, means that all of us can play some part in this basic work of our community. We should not see our cleaning and cooking duties as chores to be completed as quickly as possible, but as acts of love and worship. When we are tempted to be slap-dash in these tasks, we should remember that Christ is the unseen guest whenever we come together – and so our cooking and cleaning is to make him welcome into our midst.

MINISTRY

As God in Christ came to minister to people in all their needs, we pray that we may be fellow servants rooted and grounded in his self-giving love.

We strive to order our lives in obedience to God's will, supporting one another in our various vocations.

God in his Spirit reveals the truth as we need, that we may guide each other in the way of Christ.

May we listen to one another with deference, striving to discern and express what is right for all.

God in Jesus has given us the perfect master, that we may commission others under his power to lead his people.

May we each exercise with humility and courage such authority as is vested in us, rejoicing in the wise counsel that others may give.

As God in Christ came to minister to people in all their needs . . .

In the early stages of the Jerusalem church the apostles were in charge of every aspect of the community's life; and while the numbers were relatively small, and their pattern of life was still forming, this was appropriate. But then a crisis came. The apostles, by their own admission, were unable to organise efficiently the distribution of food to the elderly widows, and there was growing discontent in the church. So they asked the members of the church to choose seven men to serve as managers; and the apostles then ratified their choice by laying hands on the new managers. This left the apostles free to give

51

their time to prayer and preaching, and to giving spiritual guidance.

In the Pachomian monastery there is a similar distinction between the two types of leadership: pastors who give advice and guidance and who are ultimately responsible for the discipline of the community; and managers who look after its practical affairs. The pastors are often older men, some living as hermits near the monastery; and each monk is under the direction of a pastor. The managers, led by the abbot, organise not only the material aspects of the community's life – the farm, the maintenance of the buildings and so on – but also its corporate worship. In the Benedictine monastery the distinction is less marked, but still exists. Here the abbot, chosen by the whole community, is the spiritual guide; but he appoints a prior and other officers to manage various aspects of the monastery's affairs. The same distinction is also found in many ordinary churches, although the precise dividing line between different functions may vary: there is a priest or minister who is the spiritual pastor; and stewards or wardens who manage the church's material life.

During the first few years of the original community at Little Gidding Nicholas Ferrar was in charge of even the smallest detail of its life, from the worship in church to the serving of meals. But as a stable pattern formed, so increasingly he handed authority to others: one group had charge of all domestic affairs; his brother managed the estate; another group organised a study circle, and so on. By the time he died, eleven years after founding the community, the organisation was strong enough to flourish without him, and one of his nieces became in effect their pastor. So too with our community. In the formative stage one person had responsibility for the whole community. But gradually authority was devolved, and a clear distinction made between pastors who advise and guide, and managers who look after various aspects of daily life. Benedict realised that there could easily be damaging disputes and tension between the two types of leader; and for this reason he stipulated that the abbot, rather than the whole community, should appoint the various managers, thus ensuring that practical responsibility within the community derives directly from its spiritual leadership.

In the same way in our community all the members together choose the pastors; and it is they, in consultation with others, who appoint our managers.

In the story of the first Little Gidding, it is extraordinary and inspiring to see how very ordinary and even timid people grew in stature over the years, and by the time of Nicholas's death every member was exercising a valuable ministry within the community. This is the fruit of good leadership: whatever pattern and structure of leadership a Christian group may adopt, its purpose must always be to encourage and support the ministry of every person. So in our community the function of pastors and managers alike is to discern the gifts of all our members, to draw them out, and to enable them to be used in mutual service. Only in this way can our ministry truly reflect the ministry of Christ, because all of us are called to be different parts of his body.

. . . we pray that we may be fellow servants rooted and grounded in his self-giving love

When the apostles asked the Jerusalem community to appoint managers, they said that the people chosen should have two qualities: they should be full of the Holy Spirit, and they should be competent for the task. In organising the churches he founded, Paul, too, quickly realised the importance of both qualities. He rejoiced at the profusion of gifts amongst the members – there were people competent for every task that was needed; but these gifts can equally be used in the pursuit of personal power and status, and so destroy the church. So he taught that every gift should be under the rule of the supreme gift of love, which all can possess. Later, in the Epistle to Timothy, the list of qualities needed for leadership in the church are primarily moral and spiritual; and only when one is certain a person is inwardly fit, should one consider whether he has the outward gifts required.

The same theme recurs in George Herbert's advice to the Country Parson. He gently chastises those who imagine that theological expertise and a good library of books are the main qualifications for the priesthood. On the contrary, he says, the parson's library is his holy life, and his moral and spiritual example is the finest sermon he can give. We, like those whom George Herbert criticizes, will always be tempted to look for natural abilities and good training as the criteria for appointing people to positions of responsibility in the community. And it is true that without appropriate gifts and skills, our ministry will be ineffective. But without spiritual devotion those gifts and skills will be abused, and potentially be deeply destructive. Thus each of us, in wishing to use our gifts in the service of God, should first aspire to what Herbert means by a holy life.

To be holy does not mean to be dull, nor to stifle one's personality. Herbert himself loved the good things of life: music, poetry, natural beauty, and witty conversation. He had both a wry sense of humour, and a vivid imagination, as is shown in his writings. None of these gifts were jeopardised by his call to holiness, but were enhanced. While we remain gripped by self-interest, every relationship is distorted by personal rivalry, and every pleasure is spoiled by our desire to possess what we enjoy. As we grow and mature spiritually, so friendships become more peaceful and happy, and physical pleasures more satisfying.

The balance between holiness and skill is reflected in our pattern of leadership. The pastor's ministry is primarily to encourage people in the way of holiness. Much of his work is talking to people in confidence, supporting them in their discipleship of Christ. For the most part he responds to their requests for counsel, but he has the right and duty to insist on speaking to someone if circumstances demand it: holiness of life is not a luxury but a necessity in a Christian community, and the pastor must intervene when people visibly disregard its demands. The manager's ministry is to draw out people's gifts, encouraging them to develop their skills, and thence to co-ordinate their various activities within the community.

We strive to order our lives in obedience to God's will . . .

When the monk commits himself to the monastery, he vows obedience. As Benedict recognised, it is the toughest aspect

of monastic life – far harder than celibacy, for most monks –
since it hits at the heart of human sin, pride. Obedience
requires total acceptance of the monastic rule, submitting
one's will to that of the community; and, as the rule requires,
acceptance of the decisions of the abbot and other leaders.
But these outward forms of obedience, Benedict taught, must
be rooted in inward obedience to the will of God; and this in
turn requires mutual obedience, each monk trying to discern
the will of God through the insights and advice of his
brethren.

For the monk, whose life is totally immersed in the monastery, the vow of obedience embraces every aspect and every
moment of his life. For us the community is only one part of
our lives, and so our commitment is less demanding; yet
obedience is as vital to our community as it is to a monastery.
Like the monk we must each accept willingly the rule and
the pattern of our corporate life. This does not mean that we
must imagine things to be perfect; on the contrary, there are
always improvements that can be made to our way of life,
and we are each free to suggest changes. But constantly tinkering with the outward structure of the community can easily
drain our energies and divert our attention from spiritual
matters and from the service of others. So obedience to the
present rule and pattern, for all its imperfections, frees us to
concentrate on the true spiritual and practical work of the
community.

Acceptance of a rule, which is objective and whose authority is hallowed by time and usage, is the easiest part of
obedience; far harder is obedience to people. Whatever our
position in the community, each of us at times will be subject
to the authority of others, since different people have charge
of the various aspects of our life. There may be discussion
and consultation on matters of common concern, but sooner
or later those with responsibility will need to come to a
judgement – and it is at this point that the rest of us must
be obedient. Once a decision has been made argument should
cease, and each of us should play our part in implementing
the decision, regardless of whether we agree with it or not.
This will often mean following the will of someone we regard
as inferior in intellect, wisdom or experience; but the question

of whether a decision is correct is far less important than the spiritual imperative of accepting it with grace and humility.

Obedience to a rule, and obedience to those in authority, are only particular expressions of the obedience which is at the heart of all Christian life. Every person is an image of Christ, and each has spiritual gifts which embody one part of the whole ministry of Christ. And we all stand in constant daily need of his care. Thus obedience consists in receiving, joyfully and humbly, the ministry of others – to be guided, inspired, and led by the voice of Christ speaking through them.

. . . supporting one another in our various vocations

In the history of Christian community there have been three types of group. The first is the isolated or enclosed community, where the members both live and work within the community, rarely seeing outsiders. The original monasteries of Pachomius and Benedict were of this kind, and the various movements to reform Benedictine monasticism have reasserted the isolation and the strictness of their life. The second type is where all the members are dedicated to a specific work in the service of others, such as education, nursing or evangelism; and their corporate life is directed to this end. The religious orders which have flourished since the sixteenth century have been of this type; and the majority of family communities have similarly been founded to serve some special need.

The third type is when a community provides a spiritual base, supporting its members in a variety of vocations. Thus the members are involved in the world, and are free to do whatever work they choose. To a limited extent the Pachomian communities in Ethiopia have such freedom: the monks are free, if they feel called, to work outside the monastery, as parish priests or school teachers, or even in some cases in the world of business and politics. Our community is of this third type. It is open to people of any vocation, married and single, old and young. This brings two challenges which the other types of community do not face. On the one hand we must be vigilant in maintaining our corporate life, so that we find unity of spirit amidst our diversity of work. On the other hand we must support one another in our different vocations, so the community strengthens rather than constrains us in our work.

The most important work that any of us does is as a parent of children; and the raising of children should always take first place in our prayers and mutual support. While parents may have abundant love for their children, no parent has all the abilities and skills needed in the various tasks of bringing up a child; and at times every parent becomes exhausted by their responsibilities, and frustrated at the apparent lack of progress. A community can provide additional abilities to supplement those of the parents: one person may encourage the children's interest in technical matters, and in learning practical skills; another may enjoy discussing politics and history with the youngsters; another may take children camping or hiking, and so on. And all of us can at times look after children when the parents go out.

Apart from parenthood, every person's work should be treated as of equal value, regardless of its worldly status or the money earned; so every job is equally worthy of our prayers and encouragement. Those who have secular jobs outside the community may often feel cut off from events within the community; and apart from the money brought home, people may seem indifferent to what they do and the pressures they are under. So we should take particular care to keep them informed, and also try to understand the nature of their work. Conversely those whose work is largely at home or within the community can feel cut off from the wider concerns of the world, and small issues within the community can cause disproportionate anxiety. We must help every member, where possible, to have some active involvement outside the community, to complement what they do at home.

Within this diversity, our unity depends on all of us, in some small degree, sharing in our common work. There is no outside job so demanding that it leaves no time for simple cleaning and cooking; indeed such tasks can be a means of relaxation. And there is no member who does not possess a spiritual gift that can be used in the service of the community;

indeed all of us, in some measure, have the gift of loving prayer, and that is the greatest spiritual service of all.

God in his Spirit reveals the truth as we need . . .

Nicholas Ferrar's ideas of community were largely informed by his travels as a young man. He visited the Anabaptist communities in Holland where they were trying to imitate precisely the practice of the Jerusalem church. And in Italy he saw many of the new religious orders inspired by the Counter Reformation, especially the Oratories of Philip Neri, which were loose-knit communities of priests, living in a small group within their parishes and following a simple rule of life. The ideas he garnered from such disparate sources guided him in the formation of the community at Little Gidding. And once the community was established it remained open to new insights and different traditions. They invited preachers from outside; they welcomed visitors of all kinds, catholic and puritan, educated and unlearned, and encouraged the visitors to share their ideas and experiences; and they organised a study circle, the Little Academy, in which they related and discussed stories from history and classical mythology.

With our different religious traditions and experiences, we bring to the community the same broad range of ideas that Nicholas Ferrar gained through his travels. Like Nicholas, we should remain loyal to our own religious tradition, yet be open to insights from elsewhere. We must beware of wanting to defend our tradition for its own sake, or feel that our view is superior. We must become supple and flexible in mind and spirit, rejoicing in the diversity of attitudes within the community, knowing that theology and religious experience are never more than partial, imperfect signs of the mystery of God. And we should each feel free to express openly our views, even if they seem shocking or discordant; and equally be happy to change our minds in the light of the insights of others.

In addition to our various religious traditions, we come from a wide variety of social backgrounds, with different styles of upbringing and education. We should continue to respect this variety when we learn and study together in the community, using a variety of methods to suit people's tastes. There is a place for formal teaching, such as the sermon during the communion service, and it is likely that a number of members will have a gift for preaching; and there is a place too for more informal discussion on some particular topic or theme. Like the Little Academy, those who wish can meet to read drama and poetry, and to play and listen to music. And visitors to the community – even those who outwardly appear dull – will always have their own experiences and insights to share, if we are open to them. We should beware of intellectual snobbery which gives the highest place to formal education and knowledge from books. The ultimate truth is simple, and every experience, however mundane it may seem, is an opportunity to gain deeper understanding.

The fruit of open minds and hearts is that we are open to be changed as people. Like all religious groups, our community will always be prone to perfectionism, seeing ourselves as so good and virtuous compared to humanity in general that there is little need for personal change. Equally we can lapse into spiritual apathy, which appears to be the opposite of perfectionism, but has the same result: we feel so comfortable and at ease with ourselves that fresh challenges are avoided. True holiness depends on being alert to our imperfections, and willing to grow in spiritual insight. Yet, far from being grim and gloomy, such self-awareness is invigorating, stimulating our interest in fresh ideas.

. . . that we may guide each other in the way of Christ

Almost every community has been founded by someone of special vision and passion: they are often powerful and inspiring personalities, yet also beset by inward emotional conflicts from which their energy springs. Nicholas Ferrar was such a man, gifted with great insight and courage, yet never satisfied with himself, and racked by a sense of personal failure. Then, as the community becomes established, the founder must share authority, handing responsibility to those of more peaceful temperament. This transition may be painful: the founder may remain possessive of his creation, unwilling to let others make changes; and the members may feel insecure and uncertain. In the first Little Gidding Community Nicholas's death after eleven years completed the change which had already begun to happen; and his brother John and two nieces took over the leadership. Such a transition is vital, for without it the members will be stifled and their ministry suppressed. Yet it carries with it two dangers, and hence two challenges, which will always face the community, and which must be met with honesty and confidence.

The first is that charismatic leadership is replaced by bureaucratic management, which will suffocate and destroy the community. We shall always be tempted to create committees and elaborate procedures for reaching decisions, to avoid putting our trust in particular people. The motive may be pride, which makes us unwilling to invest authority in people according to their gifts; or it may be insecurity, fearing the changes that personal leadership may bring. Yet these are the very reasons why we should avoid bureaucracy, and place our trust in people. God has bestowed upon individual members the gifts we need, and we must recognise these gifts and entrust authority accordingly; if we are too proud or frightened to do this, the gifts will be wasted. And, just as the founder created the community which changed all our lives radically when we joined, so we should be willing to embrace the much smaller changes that will be required for the community to flourish in the future.

The second challenge follows from the first: that we should welcome new vision from new members. We are happy to accept the founder's prophetic vision, and even to tolerate with good humour his wilder flights of imagination, because it was he who first attracted us to the community. Yet we may stubbornly resist the prophetic vision of those who join the community later; indeed, our unspoken hostility to new insights may prevent such people joining. But if the community is to retain its vitality, and respond to God's calls in the future, we should willingly receive into membership those whom God sends with prophetic gifts; and we must be willing to be changed by their ministry.

May we listen to one another with deference . . .

In the traditional monastery the first task of the abbot is to listen, and to encourage his brethren to do the same. When the abbot calls a meeting his purpose is to listen to the opinions of the monks, and to help them to listen to each other, so that God will speak to the community through the view that emerges. Benedict urged his brethren to listen especially carefully to the younger monks, whose views can easily be dismissed by the more experienced members, since often the fresh insights of the newcomer reveal the best course. Listening is equally important in the numerous small decisions which are made each day: those with responsibility are urged to ask the opinions of other monks involved, expecting God to speak through the views they express.

The discipline of listening is astonishingly hard. Some of us tend to be strident, putting our views in a tone that brooks no opposition. Others are verbose, preferring the sound of their own voice to hearing the words of others. Some stubbornly continue to defend their opinions, long after they have been proved false; and some, perhaps the majority, want to avoid all responsibility for decisions, so they neither express their own views nor take the trouble to consider other people's. Listening to one another with care requires us to resist all those temptations. When we speak, we must be concise and succinct, and put our opinions with diffidence that allows others to disagree. We should readily change our mind if the views of others prove us wrong. And whenever our view is sought we should willingly share with those in authority the burden of making a decision.

At meetings the discipline of listening is especially vital: without it bad decisions will be made, and there will be rancour and disharmony; yet if people do listen, meetings will bring unity and common purpose. The chairman should ensure that everyone has an opportunity to speak; and if necessary he should reprimand those who are strident and verbose. When a discussion appears to be stuck and making no progress, he should call a period of silence for reflection and prayer. And he should encourage moments of humour and laughter, to release emotional pressure and to put matters in their truer perspective. Above all, we should never form small groups beforehand to agree on a united view to bring to a meeting; such factions are the enemy of true listening and destroy our unity.

The same discipline should apply in our everyday conversations on matters of common concern. It enhances both the pleasure and the efficiency of working together if we can exchange views freely, pooling our knowledge and experience. And, although one person should bear formal authority for each decision made in the community, the more we listen to one another the more equally responsibility is shared. The sign of a listening community is that formal structures are barely visible, because in practice we think and work as one.

. . . *striving to discern and express what is right for all*

Every human group has its own method of reaching decisions, which the members of the group acknowledge. In a Benedictine monastery the abbot holds absolute power, and he in turn delegates responsibility to others; thus meetings of brethren are only means through which he can consult them, asking their opinions and advice, leaving ultimate authority in his hands. In the Pachomian monastery the monks are more free: the pastors of the community only offer advice and guidance, having no direct responsibility for daily decisions; they in turn appoint the abbot and other officers, who must make decisions with the consent and approval of the members. No particular structure is necessarily superior, and different methods of making decisions will be appropriate for different forms of community. What matters is that within the structure of authority every member shares in discerning what is right for the community.

Our own structure is very close to that of the Pachomian monastery. In a community of families each must be free to order its life as it chooses; thus a strict hierarchy would be wrong. Yet like any human group we need some clear frame-work for reaching decisions. Thus, as in the Pachomian community, we choose pastors to advise and guide us, helping us to maintain unity and common purpose; they in turn appoint managers to have charge of particular aspects of the community's affairs. Each manager should try to see his sphere of responsibility in relation to the whole life of the community, and in this way carry the members with him. Before reaching any important decision he should ask the views and feelings of all who will be affected, so that they can trust him to take their needs into account.

Meetings of members are primarily for advice and consul-tation, and to share news and information. Pastors may offer reflections on some spiritual or moral matter relevant to the community, and stimulate discussion. Managers report on their spheres of responsibility, and seek the views of members on any major issues they face. At the meetings themselves we do not make decisions: rather the managers, having heard people's views, must reflect and pray, then reach their own conclusions. This both enables more efficient and caring decisions to be made, and also prevents managers avoiding awkward decisions by referring them to a meeting – a bureau-cratic device that would soon paralyse the community by interminable argument. Meetings are often tiring, and if they are held too often will make the community unduly absorbed in its own concerns. So, although they should be regular, they should not be unduly frequent.

Whatever process is used to reach decisions, the one essen-tial ingredient is prayer: at meetings, or when making decisions alone, we should be striving to hear God's Spirit speak to us. And we should remember that the Spirit is unpredictable. Thus if we are truly open to God, we should always be prepared to have our prejudices overturned and our opinions transformed: to live by the Spirit is to expect the unexpected.

God in Jesus has given us the perfect master . . .

Before founding the community at Little Gidding Nicholas Ferrar was an astute and successful businessman. He was known as gentle and considerate to those he employed, and fair to his customers. Yet he was also decisive, able to formulate bold strategies to extend the business, and at times he could be ruthless in implementing them. It was this ruthless streak which destroyed his worldly ambitions: after a major reversal in business he took bitter revenge on his opponent, even having him tried for treason; and his guilt and self-disgust for what he had done so burdened him that he withdrew from all further business dealings. Out of this emerged his desire to form a community in which he could devote himself entirely to God.

Yet paradoxically this same mixture of gentleness and firmness characterised his leadership at Little Gidding. He was patient and tolerant of people's mistakes and shortcomings, and he cared for all the members as a parent for his children; yet he was resolute and decisive, having firm ideas as to how the community should be organised, and giving clear guidance in both spiritual and practical matters. In this he was reflecting the image that Christ gives us of leadership, that those in authority should be both gates to the sheepfold and shepherds of the flock. As gates, our leaders should be welcoming, constantly seeking to draw people into the heart of the community: when people feel themselves unworthy or unloveable, the leader reassures them with his patience and love; and when they are downhearted and feel unable to contribute to the life of the community, the leader encourages and supports them in their work. As shepherds, leaders should be bold in the advice they give, offering clear vision of the way forward, both to individuals in their personal lives and to the community in its corporate life.

When things went wrong at Little Gidding or people were discontented, it was Nicholas who was blamed, regardless of where the fault lay. His sister Susanna argued constantly with him, and, although she shared his ideals, she often violently disagreed with his actions; and his brother's wife, Bathsheba, hated the life they led, and held Nicholas responsible for her misery. In this, too, Nicholas, often willingly, was having to follow the example of Christ in suffering for his sheep. The good shepherd, in Christ's image, so loves his flock that he is prepared even to die for his sheep; and the death of Christ was brought by those who felt threatened by his moral power and spiritual authority. Those called to be leaders will inevitably find they share, in some small measure, in this suffering. To the extent that they follow the example of Christ, they will threaten the moral and spiritual complacency of others, and so at times will face vicious and slanderous opposition. And if they make mistakes people may relish the opportunity to blame them. Like Christ at his trial, the leader must resist the temptation of leaping to his own defence, but should patiently accept the blame, and humbly look to himself to see how far it is justified.

To compare the leadership of the community or church to the leadership of Christ himself is to recognise that none of us is fit to be a leader. And it is this honest and heartfelt recognition which is the single most important qualification for leadership. Those who are ambitious for leadership, who want for themselves the status it confers, and who in seen and unseen ways push themselves forward, are for those reasons unsuitable, whatever other qualities they may possess. We should consider as leaders only those who are sincerely daunted at the prospect of holding moral and material responsibility for others, who will readily admit their errors and failures, and who will thus make their own leadership subservient to that of Christ.

. . . that we may commission others under his power to lead his people

Just as communities have different methods of reaching decisions, so there are different ways of appointing leaders. The first apostles were appointed directly by Jesus himself. Matthias, the apostle to replace Judas, was chosen by lot. The seven deacons of the Jerusalem church were picked by the people themselves, and presented to the apostles who ordained them. In the Benedictine monastery the abbot is chosen by the whole community: Benedict does not stipulate an election, but rather that all the members should be united in their choice. In the Pachomian monastery the pastors are chosen by the unanimous consent of the monks; they in turn propose people to manage the monastery's affairs, seeking the agreement of the members.

Since our pattern of leadership follows the Pachomian model, so too does our way of appointing leaders. Any member may propose a person as the pastor of the community, first asking whether the person will be willing to serve in this role. Then a meeting of the whole community is held at which the individual being proposed is not present. If there is disagreement the proposal may lapse, or a further meeting may be held; only if the whole community is of one mind is the person then appointed as pastor. The community may have one or a group of pastors, depending on its needs. There should be sufficient number that every member can be in close touch with a pastor; but since the pastors must at times act in unity, there should be few enough that they can be in close touch with one another. In the Benedictine monastery the abbot is both spiritual counsellor and the senior manager of the monastery, so a rare combination of gifts is needed. We, in common with the Pachomian monastery, require only the gift of spiritual counsel in our pastors.

The pastors, acting together, propose managers to have charge of each aspect of our corporate life. But, as in the Pachomian monastery, they will first speak to other members to see that the person would be acceptable as manager. In the Pachomian community it is usually younger members, with energy and efficiency, who are made managers; it is these qualities that we too should seek. The fears that people can have of giving authority to those who are young and inexperienced will be groundless if the managers trust the pastors, looking to them for advice and guidance. Hence it is vital to our well-being that pastors and managers are in harmony, their gifts and roles complementing each other.

Those we choose as leaders are fallible, vulnerable people like the rest of us. They may grow morally and spiritually in their task, or they may be oppressed by it, depending on how we treat them. If we constantly bombard them with petty demands, if we withhold information or mislead them in order to get our way, if we recriminate when they make errors of judgement, if we grumble when they take decisions we dislike, then we shall destroy their self-confidence and exhaust their energy. But if we cheerfully undertake the jobs they ask of us, if we are open and honest, if we greet mistakes with good humour, and if we willingly implement their decisions, then they shall grow in moral stature, and serve the community to the best of their abilities.

May we each exercise with humility and courage such authority as is vested in us . . .

When George Herbert became a priest he felt not only unworthy of the calling, but daunted and uncertain as to what the job involved. So he wrote his short book on the Country Parson, as a description of the task as he understood it, and as a spiritual target at which to aim. Those in our community who are called to positions of leadership will feel the same. Indeed it is right that people should regard themselves as unworthy of leading others, and feel apprehensive and uncertain of their abilities. So it is important, both for the leaders themselves and for the community, to have a clear understanding of each leader's task, and also of the limits of their responsibility.

The pastors have four specific jobs. The first is to welcome and help those who are exploring the community, to see whether it is right for them to join. Each prospective member should be under the wing of a pastor, who will correspond with them, guide their visits to the community, and share with them in trying to discern God's will. The second task of the pastors is to advise members in their stewardship: this means both speaking with each member in depth once a year about the use of their gifts and resources, and also being available to talk at other times when decisions must be made. The third task is to maintain and strengthen the unity of the community, seeking to heal rifts and to encourage mutual friendship and support. The pastor should respond at once to requests for spiritual and moral counsel, and if necessary be willing to intervene in cases of conflict between members. The fourth task is to appoint people to manage the affairs of the community.

The scope of each manager's job is defined by the pastors.

But within the limits of his responsibilities each manager must decide for himself how to tackle his job. He should set himself clear priorities, and guard his own independence and freedom of action, not allowing the urgent pressures and demands of others to divert him from what he regards as important. At the same time he should, without diffidence, ask from others the help that he needs, establishing a team of people as necessary to share his work. He should ensure that every person in the team knows clearly what is expected of them, since uncertainty soon causes tension and ill-feeling. And he should always be willing himself to do the more unpleasant and menial tasks, leading by example rather than merely issuing instruction.

George Herbert, having enjoyed a successful academic and political career in the early years of his life, was acutely aware that a country parson was in the eyes of the world a lowly occupation, held in contempt and ridiculed by many with whom he mixed. But he believed that under God the spiritual leadership of ordinary people is the highest vocation; and he regarded himself as honoured to have been called by God. It is doubtless true that to exercise leadership within our community carries no honour in the outside world, and may even invite the contempt of those who think we could use our gifts to better advantage elsewhere. And we should beware of allowing marks of privilege to infect our community, such as giving the leaders special places at community meals or in chapel, or treating them with outward deference. The honour of leadership is inward and invisible; yet we should remember that it is tiny compared to the honour simply of being a disciple of Christ – and hence being called, each in our own way, to share in his ministry.

. . . rejoicing in the wise counsel that others may give

Benedict urges the abbot of the monastery to remain constantly aware of his own weakness, remembering that a bruised reed will not be broken. And throughout his Rule Benedict reminds the monks that they have been called by God to the community, not because they are already holy, but to learn the way of holiness. This same awareness of our own weakness should infuse our life together, tempering our actions and our ministry. Whatever insights and experiences we may already have gained, whatever moral and spiritual progress we may already have made, our knowledge of God remains small and our love feeble and frail: we each have far more to learn than we have yet learned.

And so we should welcome each other's counsel and advice, and invite their criticism. We are all liable to react bitterly to any adverse judgement of ourselves, to assume that the person making the judgement is motivated by malice and ill-will. And even when we seek advice, we can feel angry if the advice does not confirm the attitudes we already hold. Yet the motives and feelings behind a person's criticisms should be of little interest to us: what matters is the truth of what they say. If we are to grow spiritually, if our knowledge of God's love is to deepen, then we must be open to the counsel and the critical judgement of others. A community in which people are able to speak the truth to one another in love, even when the truth is hard, will be spiritually alive and its members will thrive; a community where people take offence at all criticism, and so flattery is preferred to honesty, will suffocate spiritually and die.

At the end of his Rule Benedict gives fatherly advice to the monk who feels he has been set an impossible task. He should first try his best to do the work, but if he fails he should then go to his superior and confess his failure. But if the superior urges him to continue, he should trust that God will provide the necessary strength. Life in community is for all of us an impossible task: none of us is capable by our own strength of living in unity with others. Human sin is horribly persistent, and we shall grow weary of repeating the same mistakes and the same destructive patterns of behaviour. At times all of us will be tempted to despair, and look for an easier life. The truth, of course, is that there is no escape from our own sin; and the problems of community life are merely outward expressions of what is in our hearts. And once we recognise this clearly, we shall realise the difficulties and problems are themselves the lessons by which God is teaching us. Like the monk set an impossible task, we can confess to God and to our fellow members our failures; and having heard us, God will give us new strength to continue, and new wisdom to tackle the task.

RECONCILIATION

As God through the death and resurrection of his Son has reconciled mankind to himself, we pray that we may grow and mature in the image of the risen Christ.

We seek to live in harmony with one another, bearing witness to the peace to which all people are called.

God is infinitely patient in his desire for us to repent, that we in turn may be tolerant and compassionate.

May we be slow to judge the sins of others and quick to confess our own, forgiving others as Christ forgives us.

God in his mercy makes us whole, that we who are weak and foolish may proclaim his power and wisdom.

May we always be ready to open our hearts to others, reaching out to all we meet with the hand of his love.

As God through the death and resurrection of his Son has reconciled mankind to himself . . .

When, immediately after the coming of the Holy Spirit at Pentecost, Peter preached to the crowd urging them to become disciples, the one requirement was that they should repent – turn away from their sins, and direct their lives towards becoming like Christ. There were no theological doctrines to learn and believe, no specific ethical laws to accept: the only qualification for membership of the newly founded church of Jerusalem was repentance. It is this quality of repentance which should mark every Christian church and community: that the members seek to direct every aspect of their lives towards Christ.

As the Jerusalem church soon found, repentance is not a

single act, which, once accomplished, sets the person firmly and steadily on the path of Christ. We continually fall, and commit the very sins we have rejected; and, worse still, the further we go along the path, the more adept we become at deluding ourselves and others that our sins are acts of love. For this reason the early church developed a strict procedure for dealing with rifts amongst members: first the two or more directly involved should try to heal the rift between themselves; then, if this failed, one or two outsiders should be brought in; and finally the whole church should be asked to judge. The monasteries, too, soon realised the need for such procedures. In the Pachomian community it is a pastor who is brought in to heal rifts: usually the pastor speaks individually to the monks involved, giving them clear advice as to what they should do. In Benedict's monastery a monk causing division is first warned privately, and then, if he fails to mend his ways, he is rebuked publicly; in extreme cases he may be forbidden to attend common meals or even the communion.

In the wider church the importance of repentance has frequently been forgotten, or it has been regarded as a single act at one's conversion. At best this leads to spiritual apathy, the church growing luke-warm in its faith; and at worst it brings spiritual smugness, with Christians assuming that their initial repentance has placed them spiritually above ordinary humans. In the Catholic tradition, however, people have been urged regularly to confess their sins to a priest; and, although this can be reduced to an empty ritual, it has often been a deep and continuing stimulus to spiritual growth. In our community we have adopted a mixture of the Catholic practice, and that of the Pachomian monastery.

At least once each year during Lent members must set aside time for profound personal reflection: they may seek the help of a pastor within the community, or someone outside, as they feel appropriate. This is then followed by a service of reconciliation. In addition members should turn to a pastor if rifts cannot be resolved by those involved; and a pastor may, on his own initiative, intervene if he believes that people are making no effort themselves to heal a rift. Our experience constantly confirms that if we are cowardly or lax in this discipline of repentance, rifts widen with horrifying rapidity, and quickly the very heart of the community is being torn apart. Yet if we are firm and courageous in seeking forgiveness, then the bonds of love between us grow stronger than before – the sin that led to the rift becomes, through repentance, the means to new life.

. . . we pray that we may grow and mature in the image of the risen Christ

When a couple falls in love and marries, they may imagine that life together will bring unclouded happiness, and no conflict will ever darken their mutual affection. Such optimism is soon expelled as they find that within each of them there are emotional wounds and scars which are' exposed by their close relationship, and will make each want to draw back to ease the pain. They may react by bickering and nagging, driving a wedge between themselves; and so as the years pass they grow apart, sharing a house, but not sharing their hearts. Alternatively the couple may, despite the pain, be willing to look closely at their inner wounds, and find within their mutual love the means by which they can be healed. So through their marriage each grows and matures in love; and as the years pass the pleasure of their first romance is transfigured into a joy whose roots reach deep into their hearts.

The problems and the challenges of married life are writ large in community. We too can take the easy path of simply living alongside each other, meeting for worship, but with no real communication between us. There can be the outward semblance of community, but inwardly we are no more than a collection of separate individuals. In such circumstances some may simply become complacent and apathetic, their spiritual energy draining away. Others may still be filled with spiritual zeal, but prefer only private spiritual activities: going on retreats, reading spiritual literature, or practising various methods of psychological therapy. To the outsider the community may seem to thrive and flourish, especially if it organises its own retreats and programmes of therapy. But to the insider it is a place of dark loneliness, in which the activities are a futile attempt to mask the truth.

From the earliest times community life has excited people's imaginations. The story of the first community in Jerusalem or the accounts of those sturdy ascetics who trekked into the desert to form monasteries are as romantic as the finest love story. And when we join a community we can fall in love with its life and its members. If we remain loyal, then the hard reality of community life will bring not disillusionment, but fulfilment – the initial romance will be the first taste of a joy that grows ever fuller and richer. And this means we must be unfailingly honest, always willing to look at the spiritual wounds and scars which community life itself exposes; and together seek healing.

To the outsider the community in which there is true spiritual growth may seem rather dull and unexciting, since as in a marriage the mutual care and intimacy between its members will be largely unseen. But to the insider it will be a place of light, in which human love shines and stimulates new life in even the darkest corners of our hearts.

We seek to live in harmony with one another . . .

Within the first community at Little Gidding Nicholas Ferrar, like a pastor in the Pachomian monastery, was regarded as the guardian of its unity. When there were rifts or disagreements people turned to him; or, if they persisted in their conflict without seriously trying to resolve matters, he would intervene, asking to see each person in turn. Since he judged himself by the harshest standards, those who went to see him were frequently quite fearful that he would be equally harsh in his judgement of them. Yet in practice he combined high moral ideals with gentle patience at people's shortcomings, and a respect for their freedom. A meeting would typically begin by Nicholas asking clear, penetrating questions, as he sought to grasp fully the nature of the problem; and in the process of answering, the person would himself come to see things more honestly; then, either immediately or after a few hours reflection, Nicholas would offer precise, clear advice.

He made plain that the advice may be mistaken, and that the person remained free to accept or reject it. But equally in offering advice Nicholas was taking on to himself the problem the person faced, and in love and in prayer would share the struggle of trying to resolve it.

Without doubt the greatest burden that the pastors of our community carry is that of knowing and sharing the burdens of others. To listen with love, and to ask questions in order to see more clearly into a person's heart, is to lift part of the weight which burdens them onto oneself. And within a community, where the pastor is also a brother in Christ, he cannot shed his share of the burden until the whole problem is resolved. The pastor will be tempted to listen with his mind only, and not with his heart, in order to keep the person at a distance. And he will often be afraid to offer clear advice, because to do so is to play an active part in solving the person's problem, and to risk being blamed if the advice is wrong. The pastor can only listen and guide people with love if he passes the burden onto God in prayer; thus the pastor must above all be a person of prayer, prepared if necessary to spend hours each day reflecting on those in his care, and lifting them in love to God.

Yet the work of the pastor is at most only a support to the work that must be done by each one of us. When we go to a pastor for help we are not escaping responsibility for what is wrong in our lives, but asking to see more clearly what we must do. Just as the pastor may be tempted to avoid truly sharing our needs, so we too may be tempted to misuse our meetings with a pastor as a means of avoiding real action. We may give perfunctory answers to his questions, or we may simply relish the meetings as a means of focusing attention on ourselves; either way, we will be making little real effort to understand and grapple with the inward source of our difficulties. Like the pastor we too must depend on prayer, asking that we might see ourselves through God's eyes, and that the pastor should be to us a means of clearer self-knowledge.

The perfect harmony to which God calls us is a goal which we shall never fully achieve. What matters is not how near we are to that goal, or even how fast we are going towards it; God alone can judge these things. Our task is to ensure that, through prayer and the guidance of others, we are moving in the right direction.

. . . bearing witness to the peace to which all people are called

Throughout the history of the Church small communities of Christians, sharing their lives with one another, have been powerful witnesses to Christ's gospel of peace and love. In their Christian mission, the community and the parish church complement one another. The parish church, whose visible community is mainly confined to Sunday worship, cannot through its corporate life bear witness to the gospel in action; rather its task is to sustain its individual members, so that they can apply the gospel to their daily work in the world. The community, on the other hand, may have less involvement in the world, and so less opportunity to bring a Christian influence to worldly affairs; but through its corporate life, in which spiritual and material matters alike are directly subject to the teaching of Christ, it can be a visible witness of the gospel in action.

In the Jerusalem church their common life was a far more powerful attraction to newcomers than the numerous sermons the apostles preached. People were intrigued and impressed by what they saw, and wondered what could have inspired people to commit themselves to one another with such love and devotion. A few centuries later it was small groups of monks who carried the gospel to remote corners of the earth. In Ethiopia, for example, it was monks from Egypt, setting up communities and living together with such visible joy and peace, that were the foundations of the church: people were attracted by their life and came to join them, while the monks in turn set up churches in the villages. The Celtic church of ancient Britain was similar in its origins.

Our community also, in some small way, is such a witness. This is not the reason for a person joining the community; the community exists for its own sake, and we each joined because it seemed the right kind of life for ourselves. But having formed a community, we are together a small sign of the kingdom of God. And hence people will be intrigued: visitors will come wanting to know the practical details of our common life, and at times ask quite intimate questions about emotional and financial aspects of the community. Some will be critical and even rude, angry at us because we seem to threaten their own attitudes. Others will heap praise on us out of all proportion to what they have seen: they too feel threatened, and by portraying us as especially good and holy they reassure themselves that they are too frail and feeble to imitate our example. Some will try to draw us into some political or social campaign, sensing that the support of a Christian community will be a powerful boost to their cause. A few – perhaps disappointingly small in number – will be helped in their path to God, gaining fresh insight and inspiration from our witness.

Through all this we must respond with warmth and patience. We should answer people's questions honestly and fully, regardless of how often the same question has been asked before by others. We should feel neither upset at rudeness nor flattered by praise, but where possible try to help the person understand their own needs and anxieties more clearly. We should avoid becoming allied as a community to any social or political cause; rather we as individuals should willingly engage in discussion as to how the gospel teachings may apply to the issues of our time. Most of all, we should hope and pray that God may use us to help others in their faith. The questions, the rudeness, the praise, and the political discussion may all be part of people's search for God. It is not for us to judge how God may use us to speak to a person's innermost needs; and usually we will be unaware of the help we give. We should simply trust that God will speak through us as the listener needs.

God is infinitely patient in his desire for us to repent . . .

When instructing the monks on the amount of wine they should drink, Benedict remarks that ideally monks should drink none; but since it is impossible to persuade the monks of this, it is better that they should be told to drink only in moderation. The patience and realism that is contained in this instruction infuses his entire Rule. He understands the stubborness of human sin, and the futility of expecting people to behave perfectly. In a striking image Benedict tells the abbot that, when he is correcting a monk, he should not try too hard to get rid of the rust for fear that the pot itself will be broken.

For any person seeking to follow Christ, the persistence of old destructive attitudes and habits is a constant source of frustration. The new convert may imagine that the way to God is short and fast, and may despise the failings of more mature Christians; and indeed God seems to encourage new converts by giving ready answers to their prayers. But as each mile is travelled the road gets rougher and the horizon further off. So too with a community. A newcomer may at first imagine that sharing one's life with others is easy, as if it were a happy supper party indefinitely extended. But soon old habits from the past reassert themselves, and new weaknesses are exposed. The immediate temptation is to blame others within the community; and there is a perennial danger in community that particular people become scapegoats, regarded by others as the source of all problems. But we must each honestly recognise that we all share responsibility for the distorted attitudes and emotions which may beset us.

As pilgrims travelling together we must learn to be patient with the slow pace, in order to ensure that we all continue to move forwards. If one person finds another especially difficult, with conversations between them tending to cause anger and resentment, it is usually wise for them to avoid close contact for a period. Intense emotions and antagonism can dissipate our energy, and the whole pilgrimage is slowed by fruitless argument; thus it is better that the two continue travelling together with only as much contact as can remain peaceful and pleasant. Then, once hard feelings have subsided, each should pray for the other with special care; and gradually friendship will be restored.

So too when a person is frustrated at himself. While at times one is tempted to blame others for what is wrong, at others it is oneself that one holds up for contempt. Self-denigration can be as fruitless and destructive as anger and resentment towards others: every small event is turned into another source of guilt, every little failure is taken as another sign of one's own worthlessness. A person filled with self-loathing is just as unfit for the pilgrimage as one filled with anger towards others, and will hold the community back. The remedy too is similar: the person should avoid situations that evoke self-blame, and hence reduce the intensity of inward emotion, so the slow, steady progress can continue. And, to lighten the load of guilt, he should pray for the ability to laugh at himself – it is in the sound of our laughter that we hear God's reassurance that he loves us even as we are.

... that we in turn may be tolerant and compassionate

The first apostles were varied in temperament and social background, and would probably not have chosen one another as friends with whom to relax and chat. And they were as prone to petty jealousies and arguments as any group. All they had in common was that they had been called together by Jesus. Yet, through that common calling, this varied collection of people formed the basis of the first community in Jerusalem, and thence the whole church throughout the world. Through living and working together they learnt to respect one another, to appreciate one another's ideas and insights, and perhaps even to enjoy one another's company.

We too are a mixed assortment of people. There are some amongst us who are hot-headed and impulsive like Peter, while others are more sensitive and cautious like John; there are some like Philip for whom faith is easy, and others like Thomas prone to doubt even the most basic religious beliefs: there are some like Paul who have enjoyed great social privilege in their lives, while others like Mary Magdalene have had few outward advantages. In normal social circumstances we would not have been drawn together as friends, and at times we may feel intolerant of our differences. Different table manners and standards of politeness, and different political and social attitudes can evoke deep indignation and even contempt. We can, without fully realising what we are doing, pass disparaging judgements on the short-comings of others, and regard their failings as mere self-indulgence, while we happily indulge our own weaknesses. Most insidious of all we can be intolerant of the privacy of others: we can want to pry into other people's lives, feeling we have a right to know personal details about every member of the community, and react indignantly if they refuse to answer our queries.

We should learn to recognise this mutual intolerance as the evil that it is, not seeking to justify our hostility by blaming others. And we must refuse to let it mar our life together by never giving it outward expression. Then gradually, as the months and years pass, the intolerance will melt away and be replaced by mutual respect and affection. To our surprise we shall start to appreciate the friendship of people who, in other circumstances, we would barely have noticed. The difference between us in temperament and social background will cease to be a cause of division, and will be a source of mutual interest and enjoyment.

This in turn will bring the most precious fruit of community: the discovery, through direct experience, that beneath all differences we are one – and hence all humanity is one. A small community like ours is humanity in miniature: the differences between members reflect in small scale the diversity of culture and personality across the whole human race. Nations and peoples can regard each other as enemies because they can see only the differences. In our community, in which God has called together such a wide range of different people, we are compelled to look for the underlying unity, and to discover that at root we share the same hopes and fears, joys and sorrows. In this way we bear a living witness to the peace to which God calls all people.

May we be slow to judge the sins of others and quick to confess our own . . .

Benedict instructs that if a monk behaves badly he should go immediately to the abbot and confess his fault. And if a monk should become aware that he has aroused feelings of anger in another, he should at once offer an apology.

Openly and honestly acknowledging our mistakes and

wrongs, and apologising to the person who has suffered, is essential to the well-being of our community; but often it is astonishingly hard to do this. When something is amiss our strong desire is either to pretend it does not matter, or to blame someone else. And when the community is going through a difficult period, perhaps because a number of problems have arisen at the same time, there will often be an atmosphere of mutual recrimination. Benedict's instruction, if followed, would have the opposite effect: when problems arose people would willingly take the blame upon themselves.

Confession and apology is a discipline – a habit of mind and heart – which involves a series of clear steps. The first is to recognise when something is wrong. The desire to pretend that all is well arises from the fear of being blamed. We overcome that fear by realising that, whenever a person willingly takes the blame, the love and respect in which he is held increases rather than diminishes. The second step is to look objectively at what is wrong, to try and discern the causes, and hence how it can be put right. For small matters this may be easy, but often in larger matters, especially when intense emotions such as anger have been aroused, the causes may be complex and the emotions may cloud our judgement. Thus it is often helpful to talk in confidence with someone, such as a pastor, who is not directly involved, but who knows our situation sufficiently well to make a sound judgement.

The third and final step is to apologise for our fault. An apology should be simple: we should state clearly and concisely our fault, avoiding elaborate explanations and displays of emotion, and ask forgiveness. An apology should also be without conditions. Where the fault is shared it is tempting to make our apology conditional on the other person apologising; or, worse still, to use an apology as a way of putting the blame on the other person. An apology should be without 'ifs' and 'buts'.

Most important of all, an apology should be honest. The discipline of confession and apology can become so easy that people take the blame on themselves as a means of diffusing a difficult situation, and perhaps also out of a false sense of humility. The result is that within the community there will be a few people who always take the blame, while the rest are free of the discipline. While this may in the short run make life more comfortable, in the long run it saps the moral strength of the community. Honesty requires us to confess only to what we know we have done wrong.

... forgiving others as Christ forgives us

Benedict instructs that when a monk offers an apology, the one receiving the apology should simply give a blessing; and then the rift will be healed.

Forgiveness, like confession, is a discipline. While confession requires honesty of judgement, forgiveness requires imaginative honesty. When a person has wronged us, our reaction is often anger and resentment, and even a desire for revenge. Underlying these emotions is often an attitude of self-righteousness, and a sense of moral superiority. Forgiveness requires that attitude to be overturned. To forgive others is to recognise that we ourselves could have committed the same wrong, and indeed probably have done so many times in the past. It then requires a double act of imagination: first, to understand the inner reasons why the wrong was committed, and hence to feel sympathy for the other person; and second, to see oneself committing the same sin.

Granting forgiveness, like offering an apology, should be simple, honest and without conditions. The person apologising will inevitably feel vulnerable, and perhaps embarrassed, so that a few words of gratitude, and a smile or embrace, are sufficient. And we should never use the opportunity to vent our anger and resentment, for to do so would be to add our own wrong to the one already committed.

Forgiving and being forgiven are the spurs to spiritual growth. When a division between people is healed, both will have acknowledged that they are equally sinful and capable of doing wrong; and thus they become united in a common desire to do what is right in the future. When a person asks forgiveness, he is openly acknowledging his own weakness; and when a person grants forgiveness, he acknowledges that he too shares that weakness. Thus the problems and rifts between people become, through mutual forgiveness, sources of unity and love.

The deepest agony for a community occurs when wrongs have been committed, but forgiveness is blocked by the refusal of the wrongdoer to acknowledge blame. Those who are victims may feel unable to communicate with a person who has wronged them, even with a simple smile; and those who sympathise may share their antipathy. At such times those who are aware of the situation should inform a pastor, who in turn should see each person involved, helping them to speak honestly and humbly to the other. Even then the rift may not be healed because no one will accept fault. When every effort to bring mutual forgiveness has failed, and when the problem may seem so great as to threaten the solidarity of the community itself, all those involved must agree in prayer to set the whole matter aside, and no longer speak of it. It will seem sad and wasteful, because the love which binds us will have been weakened, not strengthened. Yet in setting the matter aside, we will be reminding ourselves that our eternal unity in Christ transcends any temporal matters which may divide us.

God in his mercy makes us whole . . .

The original community at Little Gidding consisted not only of able-bodied adults, but also of the old and the sick, and of young children. A dispensary was established where herbal remedies were prepared, and a room set aside where the sick could be cared for and treated. Also three elderly women were welcomed into the community, and they were looked after by the younger members. And from the outset there were numerous children, mostly nephews and nieces of Nicholas, and the old dovecote was converted into a school room for them and the local children who wished to come.

Although it is the healthy adults who bear the greatest responsibility for the daily life of the community, the sick, the old and the young are equally essential to its spiritual wholeness. And the extent to which they play a full part in a community is the measure of its spiritual health. Thus our community must be a place where the young can grow up in peace and security, where the sick can endure their illness in an atmosphere of love, and where we each in our turn can grow old and die without any sense of being a burden to others.

Nicholas Ferrar was trained in the medicine of his time, and could supervise the treatment of the sick. Today we depend on the expertise of doctors for medical advice, but the greater part of the care of the sick needs no special knowledge. It consists in the provision of good food, warm and comfortable surroundings, and loving, steadfast friendship. Most who have suffered serious illness affirm that they benefited spiritually from the experience: the pain, perhaps even the nearness of death, gave fresh insight, and put life itself into a wider, deeper perspective. Thus in caring for the sick we all can share this benefit, and learn from their experience; so even in sickness a person continues to contribute to our common life.

The first Little Gidding community had the example of Mary Ferrar, Nicholas's mother, who grew old serenely and peacefully. As she became physically less capable, she devoted more time to prayer and meditation. She loved the company of children, and spent each morning in the schoolroom encouraging their work. And she enjoyed welcoming visitors, happily answering their questions while the younger members got on with their work. Sadly we do not all grow old in this way: some resent their failing abilities, and grow petulant and manipulative, trying to force their way on others. Yet this in part can be due to the situation in which so many old people find themselves, alone for much of the day, dependent on the grudging help of others, and unable to give in return. A community can provide a context in which the old can give and receive in equal measure. The young can often talk more freely to an older person, knowing that they listen with the wisdom of experience and that they pose no threat of rivalry. The elderly in the community are its anchor, holding it steady in times of emotional and spiritual storm.

The most important members of the community are its children. They are the most vulnerable, and they in the course of their lives have the most to contribute. A child's greatest need is for a stable and secure family; and so the community must do nothing which threatens family life, and do all it can to support it. Here too the elderly can often help, looking after the children to give parents a rest, and encouraging the children in their work and play. At our communal meals children should always be welcome, even if it means some disruption to the adults; and we should where possible draw them into our conversation. And although many of our services will be inappropriate for children, we should ensure that there are some in which they can fully participate. Children teach as well as learn: even the naughtiest child reminds us of our ultimate calling as Christians, to be like little children to our heavenly Father. To watch an infant play, and to share in his game, can be an act of worship as profound as the Lord's Supper itself.

. . . that we who are weak and foolish may proclaim his power and wisdom

It has always been easy to regard monks and nuns as especially holy, called to live by higher standards than the rest of us. Their vow of celibacy and their adherence to a strict rule of life seems to make them different from married people who are free to live as they choose; and we can readily imagine that monks and nuns are above the temptations and emotional problems which beset ordinary people. The passage of time has given a similar glow of holiness to Nicholas Ferrar and George Herbert and their respective households: we assume that the steady rhythm of their life and worship was unmarked by conflicts and disputes. As a result, although we may admire such saints, we can comfortably conclude that their example has little relevance to our more normal existence.

Our community can be regarded with the same misapprehension. Outsiders imagine that only people who are especially devout and righteous could live in a Christian community; and that exceptional spiritual and moral strength is required of its members. They may even think that there is some special expertise – some skill or training – which is needed.

The truth is quite the reverse. In joining a monastery a monk gains no spiritual advantage, and remains as prone to temptation as before. Nicholas Ferrar and George Herbert were both men who suffered continual self-doubt, and it was frustrated political ambition that drove them both to a life of prayer. We too enjoy no special wisdom and strength, and as individuals there is nothing to distinguish us from any other members of the human race. Yet, far from being a handicap in our life together, this ordinariness is vital to our common calling. Individually we are weak and foolish, but together we find strength and wisdom. Each of us is weak in some respects, and strong in others; foolish in some respects, and wise in others. In coming together as a community our different strengths and insights complement one another, so in our unity we can guide and sustain each other.

In past centuries God called thousands upon thousands of men and women into monasteries and convents; and despite the abuses and the corruption into which some of these communities fell, they formed the spiritual heart of the medi-aeval church. Today God is calling thousands upon thousands of families and single people alike into communities such as ours, to be the spiritual heart of the Church of the future. Yet many may be deaf to the call because they imagine they are unfit for such a life. We must never allow our own spiritual pride to support such an error, by suggesting that we ourselves are special, or by hiding our faults. God calls ordinary people to be disciples of Christ; and from amongst these he calls ordinary people to belong to communities. Only by remembering our weakness and folly as individuals can we bear witness to the miracle of Christ's love, that together we find extraordinary strength and wisdom.

May we always be ready to open our hearts to others . . .

Benedict urges his monks to welcome each guest as if he were Christ himself; and throughout his stay at the monastery the guest should be treated with the greatest respect. Yet Benedict knew that the monastery's hospitality could be abused by people pretending to be devout Christians, but who in fact simply wanted free food and shelter or, worse still, desired to corrupt the life of the monastery. In such cases hospitality should be refused. The Ferrars at Little Gidding, despite their desire to be hidden from the world, soon became well known and visitors would arrive in large numbers. They were anxious that they would be overwhelmed by the demands of hospitality, so they decided that if a person arrived without a prior arrangement he was given food and drink, and then sent on his way. The Ferrars enjoyed their guests, and appreciated their ideas and the news they brought; but bitter experience made them wary of people who came as spies, in order later to spread slander about the community.

In our community, where we live as separate households, guests must be cared for by individual families, rather than by the community as a whole. Thus the extent to which we can receive guests depends on the willingness and ability of particular families to look after them. Some families, perhaps with small children and with little spare space in their house, may be unable to welcome guests, apart from their own relatives and personal friends. Others, on the other hand, may choose to live in a house too large for their own needs, in order to have room to receive guests. The community should appoint someone to take charge of guest arrangements, allocating those who wish to stay to particular households.

We too should try to welcome all guests as if they were Christ. Often guests have much to give to the community through sharing their experiences; yet we, like all communities, are vulnerable. The family must not allow itself to have so many guests that its personal life is overwhelmed; it is better to refuse additional guests than threaten the family life of the community. More especially the type of people who abused Benedict's and the Ferrars' hospitality are still to be found; and we should try to exclude them. There are those, often deeply disturbed psychologically, who wander from place to place, demanding not only food and shelter, but limitless personal attention. Some families may be willing to receive such people for a period in the hope of helping them; but often nothing is gained, and a great burden placed uselessly on the family. Worse still, there are those who want to pry and find scandal, and enjoy creating tension and division within the community; such people should be turned out immediately, since they can do severe damage.

When receiving guests into our homes we must strike the right balance between caring for their needs, and giving them freedom. Some come simply to rest, and may want to be silent or go out on long walks. Others are searching and exploring, and want to talk about our life and faith; we should try to arrange for such people to meet various members of the community who may be helpful. We should give our guests clear information about the times of meals and prayers, and how they can make refreshments, and help them plan their stay to suit their needs. Thereafter we should get on with our own normal daily lives. If we are relaxed and at ease in receiving guests, then they shall feel comfortable and enjoy their stay; if we fuss over them, they shall feel awkward and tense. During the period of their stay we should treat our guests with the same love and affection as we treat each other, regarding them as our brothers and sisters.

. . . reaching out to all we meet with the hand of his love

A person's motives for joining a community are mixed and various. For some it is a simple, logical step forward in a smooth progress through life. For others a crisis in their personal lives or careers leads them to look afresh at their hopes and ambitions; and joining the community is the outcome of that review. The desire for a loving environment in which to raise children or to grow old is often important; and even losing a job or having problems with marriage can lead, in an unexpected way, towards community life. Yet all of us, regardless of our circumstances, are looking to the community to provide spiritual, emotional and material security.

That sense of security is both a precious, and also a most dangerous gift. It is dangerous if it causes us to withdraw from worldly concerns, cutting ourselves off from the wider church and society, so that we mix only with other members of the community. Yet it can be an invaluable gift if we derive from it the strength to reach out to the world, to deepen our care and concern for the needs of others.

We should each be involved with the neighbourhood in which we live, and especially the local church. We may find that our own worship within the community is so satisfying that going out to church feels unnecessary. But, while in the short run this may seem harmless, in the long run it will cut us off from the larger body of the Church; and, worse still, it may engender a sectarian snobbery which regards our own worship as spiritually superior to that of an ordinary parish church. All of us should be committed members of a local church, sharing fully in its worship and fellowship. We should also join local clubs and societies according to our various interests, and our children should mix freely with those nearby. Within the neighbourhood we should avoid operating as a community, but rather involve ourselves as individuals: if the community is seen as a single entity with a common mind on all matters, local people will feel threatened and hostile; but if we are seen as separate individuals, with normal cares and concerns, trust and friendship will grow naturally.

When Nicholas Ferrar came to Little Gidding, he hoped to withdraw from the world of politics in which he had once been so ambitious. Yet any community in which people share their lives, spiritually and materially, is itself a living political statement about how society should be organised. Thus Little Gidding was the object of fierce debate, even to the extent of its opponents presenting to Parliament a petition to have the community forcibly closed. We too may hope that our community can insulate us from the world of politics; and, if so, we too shall be disappointed. We may be spared the concerted opposition that the first community faced, but we cannot avoid others drawing political implications from our way of life. Some amongst us may have the capacity to engage in political debate, and to derive from experience in the community insights and ideas that are relevant to the social and economic issues of our time. Others will have little ability and appetite for such discussion. But all of us can share in the most practical and powerful political activity known to man: praying with all our hearts that God's kingdom may come on earth; and praying that in some small way our community may be a seed of that kingdom.